Masked

Masked

The unbelievable Harry Bensley

DUNCAN SAY

SLEIGHT BOOKS
ESSEX, UNITED KINGDOM

This book is a work of fiction based upon the life of Harry Bensley

In some cases the names of people, places and events have been changed or invented

Artwork by the author with help from Alan Brown

Typeset by Pressbooks

Printed by IngramSparks

Published by Sleight Books

To Sylvie
who gave me the time and space to make this happen.

I first met Harry Bensley in an article in my local paper headlined 'Mystery man walked round the world and ended up in Essex'. Harry walked off the page and into my life.

Sometime later I purchased this postcard, one of the very first souvenirs of the Iron Mask and his assistant. Sadly, it was never posted, so there is no record of where or when the purchaser met the Iron Mask. It is both a fact and mystery, like so many of the events in this book.

Prepare to meet Harry Bensley. As we will see the Mask hid much more than just his face.

News of the Iron Mask

With his face concealed behind a black iron mask and pushing a perambulator before him, a mysterious figure left Trafalgar Square the other morning for a walk round the world. He is starting penniless and will subsist solely by selling photographs and pamphlets. He expects to be back in ten years.

Aberdeen People's Journal, January 11, 1908

The man in the iron mask has got into difficulties on his first day's travels. Yesterday he was at Bexley Heath, charged with hawking without a license. If the magistrate compels him to unmask he has lost his wager.

Lancashire Evening Post, January 4, 1908

In the privacy of his room he had removed the iron mask, but his head and face were shrouded in a black cloth, giving him an inquisitorial appearance that was somewhat weird; and the Press man's creepy feeling was not lessened by the assurances that the 'unknown' though quite invisible himself could see him quite clearly.

Hastings and St Leonards Observer, February 1, 1908

Penzance has received a visit from that mysterious person who has become world famous as the "Man in the Mask," and the conditions of whose remarkable wager created such a sensation when first published ... his conversation betrays that he is a man of considerable education and culture.

Cornishman, April 9, 1908

"It is immaterial what the weather is like to me. I walked into Poole covered in snow, you could hardly see me ... but I always push through whatever the weather."
Berkshire Chronicle, May 20, 1908

Whereabouts is the Man in the Iron Mask? Readers may remember that two years ago he started from Trafalgar Square, having undertaken to walk round the world...
Akaroa Mail and Banks Peninsula Advertiser (New Zealand) February 24, 1911

PART 1

Begin at the end

Dad

Doncaster, Easter 1977

In the walnut sideboard in the back room, there is a battered red tartan shortbread tin which had long been the resting place for old family passports, birth certificates and the television license. Under the tin was a hard black leather case and within that a Philips cassette recorder. As Gill picked it up she wondered if the batteries had died as she could not recall when it had last been used. She pressed the chunky central lever forward and watched as the needle on the meter moved into the green. That was one problem solved, she thought. Now she only had to worry about how the machine worked.

Gill took the microphone, slotted it into its flimsy plastic stand and placed it on the coffee table in front of her Dad who was watching with a bemused smile. He had folded the magazine which had inspired this unusual activity so that the article was held open. Then she connected the din plug into the side of the recorder. Her eldest son resentfully handed her a pristine Scotch C90 tape from his room which he had bought in town that morning and was intending to use to record a Derek and Clive album borrowed from the central library.

Gillian wrestled with the case, peeling away short darts of cellophane which stuck to her fingers. Once freed of its covering, she inserted the cassette into the slot, closed the lid and pressed the central lever forward while holding down the red record button.

'Can you say a few words, Dad?'

'What do you want me to say?'

'Tell me about your journey up.'

'We drove up in the car love and there was a lot of traffic, always is on a bank holiday weekend.'

Gill watched the needle and adjusted the recording dial to make sure the level was just so.

'That's enough Dad. I'll just replay it, make sure it sounds all right.'

She spun the tape back and pressed play. Her Dad's voice came through clear as a bell.

'Okay, Dad, ready when you are.'

TAPE 1 – SIDE 1

This was years ago mind, 1956 if I remember right but there had been this piece in the morning newspaper and I was tingling all over the minute I read it. It was just like the Reader's Digest article here. Straight away I knew this was him, the man that mum had told me about. To find out he was still alive and what's more not far from me, well, that was it. I just had to go and see him. I took some time off work, gathered up your grandma's old souvenirs and was on the first train I could catch down to Brighton.

It was a cold March afternoon. Along the seafront the wind was whipping up the waves and there was spray in the air as I walked to the hospital. When I got there of course it wasn't visiting time and the matron was pretty shirty about it but I put my foot down and said I had come a long way. She gave way and let me see him for the first time. I didn't have to ask which one was him because it was like looking at my older self. He was stocky of build, although the old green paisley dressing gown he was wearing looked much too large for him, which suggested that he had lost a lot of weight. His hair was similar but grey and he had the same squarish face as me. I've got his nose, for better or worse and I'll never forget he was playing cards.

I walk up, bold as, and say, 'Harry? Harry Bensley?' Because that was the first time I genuinely knew his name. He looked up at me with a big smile.

'Are you the Chaplain's friend? I've been waiting for a partner for a hand or two.' His eyes twinkled as he spoke. 'I'll warn you though, I've got a streak on today.'

I was on the back foot because his voice came as quite a shock as he spoke so respectably.

'No, you don't know me.'

'Introduce yourself then. It's not good form to keep a secret.'

Then I remembered that mum said he was a bit of a toff and pulling myself together I said what I had come to say.

'Well, it seems that I am your son, Jim.' I am smiling and holding my hand straight out for him to shake. I study him closely and I can tell that this has not ruffled him one bit. He had some front that old boy. He ignores my outstretched hand and instead brings his hands together while still holding some of the cards. Then he looks up at me and says with a bit of a smile, 'That is a remarkable claim, Jim, especially as the last time I did a family headcount you were somewhat conspicuously absent.'

I will be honest Gill love, I had wondered on the train how this meeting would start, so I thought it was time to bring out my trump card, if you will. I had wanted to wait and get to know him but now was the time to act. I delved into my bag and brought out one of mum's postcards and then placed it down on the table in front of him.

'This lady is my mother Mabel and this photograph is proof that you both met.'

It was a photo like the one here in the article but this has your grandma in a large hat and she's flanked by the two gentlemen. I've looked at it all my life and wondered what the truth of it was. These two chaps, one with a knight's helmet covering his head and both wearing polo-neck jumpers with 'Walking Round the World' embroidered on them. Then between them, there is that strange perambulator and a big sign at the front saying, '£21,000, the biggest wager on record'.

He says, 'Interesting postcard but I don't see myself in the picture.'

'Don't you wriggle, that's you in the mask. I read it in the paper.'

'In a newspaper?'

'The Daily Mail, I've got it here. It's an article about you being taken unwell and when I read it I knew I had to meet you.'

It was peculiar because there was a trace of a smile on his face which I felt he was trying to suppress but I had got through his defences.

'So how is Mabel?' he says.

'She died nearly thirty years back but I'm sure she would be glad of you showing an interest, after all the effort you made at the time to keep in contact. I thought you'd be long dead too.'

'I'm sorry to disappoint you in still being flesh and blood but they are trying their best to finish me off in here. Aren't you Matron?'

He raised his voice and Matron sat at her desk in the centre of the ward shot a resigned look back.

'Quiet now Mr Bensley, there are patients trying to rest.'

I wanted to get Harry back on the subject so I mentioned something I had read in the paper.

'They said you were a rich man.'

Harry glanced speculatively at me and then chuckled.

'Bit of a gold-digger, are we? Listen up then, the family was rich but that is all history because my father invested it all in Russian Bonds and the revolution took all his money a long, long time ago. So if you have come looking for your inheritance, you would be better off sending a letter to Stalin. He's a pretty even-handed understanding fellow, I hear.'

'Stalin died,' I said, 'some time ago.'

'You would receive the same answer, I'm sure.'

I could feel Harry's eyes exploring my face, trying to read my reaction but I was not surprised. I hadn't come looking for money, he was my reward.

He lent forward and whispered slowly. 'What do you know about this?'

'Mum had these pictures you see here and when I was about fifteen she told me that the man in the mask was my father but that was it, not a word more. Nothing about how you met, who you were or anything really. I didn't like to ask and she wasn't one to tell. For years I've not known if you are real or a figment of my mum's imagination and it wasn't until reading the newspaper article that I could start to believe that you really existed. So I've come here to hear the truth about you and what happened back then.'

'You feel that I am obliged to tell you the truth. The truth is a very strange tale, you may find it fanciful.'

'It's all odd, the picture, the story in the paper.'

At last Harry put down the cards, his chest rose and he gave out a long and deep cough that he had probably been trying to suppress for a while. This was followed by several more that caused his whole body to shake and shudder. They never told me what his problem was but I would guess it was pneumonia. Finally the spasms of coughing ended and Harry dabbed his face with a white cloth handkerchief, composed himself and began his incredible story.

'Those days, the best days, I'll never forget. I might misplace my glasses but the memories remain.' He tapped his brow with his index finger.

'A large country house, nannies, servants and all the privileges of wealth. Imagine, the lawns stretch to the far horizon on all points of the compass and you get the picture. My father had these lands and investments and as a young boy I wanted for nothing, except adventure and excitement.

'At the age of five I was sent off to join my older brother at boarding school. We came home for the holidays and would pass the time playing games. There were some suits of armour in the Hall and as we were growing up we found that these suits were about the right size for us to wear. It was great fun to put them on, clank around the garden and be one of King Arthur's knights of the round table, or fighting the French at Agincourt for King Harry and England. These were the very best of times when I was young.

'After school I went to university but that wasn't for me. I was not academic, nor was I much of a sportsman and I found it all a bit of a bore. Eventually father relented and set me up with a trust fund. I moved to London, found an apartment in the West End and joined a club. I spent a few years in this idyll at the turn of the century. That was a time for living.

'One particular evening after a profitable day at Ascot racecourse I was invited to a ball at the Dorchester. I went back to my apartment, dined and changed into my best evening wear and most comfortable dancing shoes. It was about eleven o'clock that I arrived by carriage and was recognised by several of the young ladies. I can't move so well today but back then I cut quite a dash on a sprung floor and many were eager to have at least one dance with me.

'Inside, let me tell you, the ballroom was the most marvellous place. The music lilting and swooping around the room and all the sashaying ladies in their elegant silk ball gowns, the gentlemen and officers in close attendance often in their most flamboyant uniform. The air filled with the frantic rumour and intrigue of the season in mid-flight.

'I may have lacked the peacock finery of many in the room, however I was very much in demand, because although this might sound immodest, I commanded the floor. Other couples could dance but the spotlight would always fall on us. There was no great secret, to dance with style and grace you must not only be in tune with your partner but also with the rhythm of the whole ballroom. My skill was an awareness of the movements of the other couples and careful negotiation of the space that ebbs and flows on the floor.

'Or at least that was how I perceived my abilities. Behind my back another couple had swayed too close, we touched and before I knew it I had lost my footing and I was tumbling across the floor. The gentleman was quick to lend a hand to help me to my feet but I realised that I had turned my ankle so I bowed to my partner and awkwardly made my way off the dance floor to find a seat.

'It was at this point that I was met by a man who was the father of one of my pals at the club. I fancy you may have heard of him, the Earl of Lonsdale. Why he was here at the ball I cannot say but he was sharing a table with a silver-haired gentleman upon whose face was such an alarmingly large red nose that it took all my efforts to prevent me from staring. The Earl asked me to join them at their table. This was not my idea of a gay evening but as I cannot dance anymore, the opportunity of a rest is too good to miss. I sat down and within moments my next dance partner sought me out.

'I'm sure I'm next on your card, Harry.' She says but before I can reply the Earl of Lonsdale chips in.

'I am sorry but Mr Bensley is a bit busy at the moment.'

'This is intriguing as I am just taking a breather before tentatively testing my foot but obviously these two gentlemen desire my undivided attention.

'Harry Bensley, I would like you to meet J. Pierpont Morgan, Pierpont to his friends. Pierpont this is Harry Bensley. We were just talking about you.'

'JP Morgan, the name has a familiar ring. Could it be that I am sitting with the famous American Steelmaker and Banker? I am astonished to be a third of such exalted company. JP Morgan was one of the world's richest and most powerful businessmen, the 5th Earl of Lonsdale was one of the most influential sportsmen. I, in comparison, am a complete nobody. Or at least I should have been thinking this but for the fact that I was still massaging my ankle.

I reply, 'Delighted I am sure but I can't imagine what brought me to your attention.'

'At this point JP Morgan turned towards me and forced his features into a smile, an effect that was difficult to achieve below his extraordinarily bulbous nose. Then he spoke with the most mellifluous Boston accent.

'I have never danced due to an affliction when I was young Mr Bensley but we were both admiring your dancing. You certainly know how to steer your way across a dance floor and your partners demonstrated much more grace when in hold with you. We observed you carefully and it was remarkable how they improved in your arms. However it was a shame that the young lady tripped you and quite deliberately I can tell you. She leaned her leg across a long way to hook yours. If this ball was adjudicated she would be sitting down for the rest of it!'

'Call me Harry, please. I suppose it is the price you pay. There is some cut and thrust on the dance floor and I fear I may have let down her older sister a season or two back. We walked out together for a while. I shall need to be more careful in future. Thank you for your kind words about my dancing. I think it is nerves that do it for some of my partners, it can be quite daunting on the floor with everyone watching but knowing that I, well, I don't normally have an upset like that, so they relax and then we can just dance.'

'The Earl held up an enormous cigar and attracted the attention of a passing waiter.

'Could you have this cut for me and bring a taper to light it. Maybe some brandy and soda for the three of us,' he glanced around and seeing us nod in agreement, he added, 'And leave the decanter.'

JP Morgan took up the conversation. 'While we were admiring your dancing, we were saying how much closer the world is these days, Mr Bensley.'

'I found this all very perplexing and what they thought I could contribute to this conversation beyond mere agreement completely baffled me. The Earl, took up the thread.

'So we were toying with ideas about how to make a round the world journey more demanding, give it some glamour so to speak for today's public.'

'The waiter brought the brandy and soda and I went straight to it, an hour or so of dancing can give you a terrific thirst. Thankfully my hosts weren't offended by my haste and as the Earl was busy carefully lighting his cigar with the taper, JP Morgan picked up the conversation. The steel magnate sat forward.

'Think back a few years when that book came out, "Around the world in eighty days". That was just a fiction of course but the record is now just over 54 days and that is held by an American I'll have you know. The Phileas Fogg thing is old hat these days. It needs some razzmatazz.'

'That's exactly it, Pierpont old fellow,' said the Earl as the smoke from his cigar swirled around him. 'The journey needs a bigger challenge. Travelling is not enough. Physical endeavour, muscle power, that's what it lacks. Walking and swimming, now there's a test.'

'Come on Hughie,' said JP. That was the first time I'd ever heard an Earl being referred to by his first name and I was somewhat taken aback by the idea that it was still in common use. 'It's *travel* round the world, not swim it. So what about, you must walk but you can use regular shipping lines to go from continent to continent, say.'

'For the first time in this strange conversation I felt the urge to join in. I was on to my second brandy and soda by this time and I was beginning to feel revived.

'What about an itinerary, places that the challenger would have to walk through and maybe collect some proof on arrival?'

'JP Morgan looked at me with a speculative eye.

'The challenger eh? So you are suggesting documenting the passage, of course that would be a necessity. I like your thinking Mr Bensley, you're a practical man and in this age we need practical men, don't we Hughie? Let's take a table in a restaurant and discuss this further.'

'With this we got up to leave. Several ladies on my dance card approached to ask me where I was going and I replied that I could dance no more that evening. Normally I would have danced in the ballroom until the dawn broke but tonight somehow was different, without a doubt something momentous was going to come of it.

'I collected my hat and coat and we took a hansom cab to Dolaros, a late night supper bar in Percy Street. The Earl asked for a table where we could speak freely and after a little discussion they took us to a private room upstairs. We could still hear singing and laughter from the main restaurant as Dolaros was a popular meeting place for actors from the nearby theatres after the curtain had fallen. First came the red wine then some food as we continued the conversation.

'The Earl had the first truly unusual idea. 'He should push a perambulator the whole way.'

'That caused us all to laugh heartily.

'Really, and what would be the purpose of that?' asked JP.

'The Earl looked affronted and then replied as if it was obvious. 'To carry his worldly goods of course. It's a very practical suggestion.'

'In its own way I suppose it was. By this time we were a very merry party and the suggestions were coming thick and fast with the Earl leading the conversation.

'He should start with only a pound in his pocket and have to pay his way around the world.'

'A budget, that is a very important detail, so how will our challenger make a living?' said JP.

'Again I found my voice, I was beginning to get the hang of this peculiar idea. 'He could sell things, souvenirs and the like to people he meets. It could be most successful.'

'I could tell this comment had made quite an impression on my companions as the Earl called for the port and passed it around the table.

'I've got a corker,' said the Earl, enveloped in the blue smoke of his latest cigar. 'Oh, yes this would be the coup de grace. He must remain anonymous for the whole trip. He must not show his face or reveal his identity for the entire journey.'

'Wouldn't that be impossible?' JP said.

'And,' ignoring JP's comment, the Earl smiled broadly as he tapped the grey ash from the end of his cigar into the tray as if to reinforce his point, 'he should find a wife and marry her along the way. There, I think we've got every condition covered.'

'I was incredulous, 'No one would accept such a challenge. Why should they when it would be so difficult?'

'JP Morgan gave a long sigh and looked down. Then he said, 'Because. No wait, there has to be an answer. What was the wager in that damn Jules Verne book?'

The Earl said, 'Twenty thousand pounds behind the bar of the Reform Club if I remember rightly.'

'There it is then, the wager shall be one hundred thousand dollars. What's that in your sterling?'

'That would be a tidy purse. About twenty-one thousand pounds.'

'Excellent, there we are. I think our work is done. Now all we need is a challenger. Obviously it would be beyond the abilities of any Englishman.'

'I had kept quiet but now it was my time to speak. I drew myself up and said, 'When would you like me to start?' and with that they all fell about laughing.'

The Matron interrupted the conversation. 'I think that's enough talk for now Mr. Bensley, you need your rest. Mr. Beasley, is it? You should come back at visiting time, you'll find the information on the notice board at the entrance of the ward.'

I told Harry I was staying at a local b&b and would be back the next day and he said he was looking forward to it. Then he asked if I could come in the early afternoon as his wife visited in the evenings and I said that would be fine.

(END OF SIDE 1)

Visit

Brighton, March 21, 1956

The sun dips low behind the bare armed trees that gently sway in the freshening wind as Kate makes slow progress along the road to the hospital. Each winter for years now Harry had experienced terrible bronchitis but this year the illness had come late, the winter had passed and he had been well, up until now. Kate thought of years gone by, time was that Harry would have convalesced in his own bed, especially as the cost of medical treatment would have swallowed all of their savings. So Kate was grateful that the hospital had taken him in.

As she walks up the steps of the entrance, Kate reflects that this gratitude does not extend to affection towards the hospital. Hospitals she feels, make her uneasy and it was not just the antiseptic smells but the medical staff who expect order and respect. As she enters the ward there is a throng around the large mahogany desk, where the nurses and white coated doctors are writing notes and the queen of all this industry is the Matron.

'Oh, Mrs Bensley, your Harry's had a visitor,' says Matron with a knowing smile as Kate passes by. Kate glances quizzically at Matron and wonders, as none of her friends or relatives had planned a visit, 'Oh, yes, who was that then?'

'Not one of his usual visitors, it was a man.'

That's enough for Kate, she bustles up the ward as fast as her legs can carry her because this is something new. Kate bends down and gives Harry a light kiss as they always do when greeting.

'I hear you had company this afternoon.' She says and Harry replies with a mischievous smile, 'I thought you might, I'm not sure who he was though.'

'Didn't he introduce himself, then?'

'Yes, Jim Beasley, he said he saw an article in one of the papers about me.'

Kate laughs. 'You always said you wanted to be famous.'

'I did, didn't I? The thing is, he's turned up because his mother claims that he's my son. He has a picture of me with his mother together on the road when I was doing the challenge.'

'What's all this then? Is this that wife you left on the road? Don't tell me she's come looking for her allowance at last.'

'Oh, she would be out of luck on that count, my sweet, wouldn't she just? Not to worry though, his mother died some time ago, so I have nothing to fear there. I can't be sure but I believe he just wants to hear the story about the wager. All of it. It's a few years since anyone has listened to my tale and it feels good to give it an airing. It just might be the last time I do, so I want to do it justice. Anyway he's a reasonable enough man, he's got an open face and no axe to grind. I don't think he is here to cause trouble.'

'That's a relief I suppose but it's not him I'm worried about really, my love. It's what you're going to say that causes me concern.'

Later, Kate leaves him sitting in bed with a gleam in his eye that she has not witnessed for years but as for telling the whole story. Well, no one would believe that.

Plans

Doncaster, Easter 1977

TAPE 1 – SIDE 2

The next day I needed to shield my eyes to see up the ward because the afternoon sun was shafting through the large sash windows. Harry was pleased to see me even though he didn't look any better. The nurses had given him some medicine and tidied him up a bit, combing his hair and straightening him up in bed to make him more presentable. Harry couldn't wait to get started.

'Yesterday I told you that I accepted the challenge but the first thing I have to say is that it wasn't the drink talking, although a fair amount of what was said that night was aided by the alcohol. No, I'll tell you my motive. Up until this point in my life, what had I been? There were plenty of events in the social year for a man such as myself to be amused and entertained but I always felt that something was missing, some purpose, some reason and now this challenge arriving as it did out of the blue offered me the chance to do something remarkable, to be somebody.

At the same time I was aware that I may not have been chosen at random. To these two powerful men I was a plaything, I have no idea why they chose me, maybe I epitomised all the flawed characteristics of modern youth and they wanted to see if I had any depth, any character. Beyond that I cannot say but I was determined to prove that there was more to me, that I did indeed have pluck and stamina.

We parted and agreed to meet again in a month. They went away to set out the conditions, I to begin my preparations.

That was difficult because I quickly realised I could tell no one, I could involve no one, even beginning to plan the challenge was in itself a challenge. I took on an alias and rented a lock-up away from the centre of town from where I could plot the journey and stockpile the necessary equipment. Most difficult of all I had to find a way of telling my family I would be away for several years.

A few weeks later I received a summons to meet the Earl at the Sportsman's club in London. On arrival I was taken to a private room, the walls of which were full of bookshelves, the books themselves a mere ornament. In the centre of the room above the table was a brass lampshade that emitted a pool of electric light, illuminating the green leather top. Three small sheaves of papers were carefully placed around the edge of the table with blotting paper and pens. The Earl and JP Morgan sat together and I took, when offered, the only empty chair. JP Morgan began the conversation in a solemn tone.

'Englishman, I hope you are ready for this but I don't believe for one minute that you are. We have drawn up the requirements for the wager and we've had a lawyer ensure that it is watertight. We have set out a series of conditions that you will find numbered on the papers in front of you. So let us start with page one from the top. This is the whole challenge. To walk round the world, masked, pushing a perambulator.'

I nodded.

'That is clear then. Condition two, to remain masked and entirely unknown throughout the whole journey. Agreed?'

'Yes, of course.'

'Condition three, to be allowed to sell photographs and pamphlets while on the journey.'

The Earl then began to talk. 'This next one is mine. Condition four, to be allowed to expend any sum not exceeding one pound sterling for photographs and pamphlets for sale at start. We can't have you using your inheritance to get around the world. You have to earn it.'

'Condition five,' continued JP 'to start from Trafalgar Square, London, on the first day of January 1908 at ten thirty am. Condition six, to call at the capital and three other towns named in the appended list, in each county in England.'

The Earl held up a sheet of paper from the pile. 'This here is the appended list.'

'Condition seven, to obtain a document, signed by the mayor, or any responsible person certifying that you arrived at the place mentioned therein and the date thereof. Condition eight, to obtain the postal stamp of every town passed through on your journey. Condition nine, all expenses of the journey to be defrayed by the sale of the photographs and pamphlets above mentioned. Condition ten, to wear the mask at all times whilst walking and in all public places. Condition eleven, apparel to be worn at the start to consist of the following articles: one suit of clothes, one pair of stockings, one shirt, one under-vest, one pair of pants, one pair of boots, one pair of puttees, one jersey, one handkerchief, one mask.'

'Condition twelve, to find a wife on the journey.'

That made me sit up. 'Hang on,' I said, 'I didn't think you were serious when you mentioned that.'

'You are not married, are you Mr Bensley?'

'No, certainly not.'

'Then this will be an opportunity for you as you travel the world. Think of all the women that you are going to meet, once they hear that you are eligible, well, just imagine.'

'Condition thirteen, to forward an account of the miles walked and towns visited with all the necessary documents from the capital of each county and all other towns mentioned in the appended list.'

'Condition fourteen, to visit the countries of the world in the order of the appended list.'

'Condition fifteen, to be allowed to go as you please.'

'Condition sixteen, all the above conditions must be strictly adhered to, otherwise the above wager will become null and void. Obviously we need to make sure that you comply with all these conditions so in order to ensure this we have one further stipulation.'

The Earl leaned forward, 'Yes, it's all very well getting stamps from all these places you visit but how will we know when you are in Timbuktu or wherever, that you really are on your feet and aren't being carted around in a sedan chair or on the back of some elephant?'

JP Morgan then continued, 'So, we have taken on the services of an assistant for you. This person will watch your every step, collect the documentation as you go and send us reports of your progress but you will be responsible for his daily outgoings. Finally young man, there must be some jeopardy for you. So if you fail to complete this task, which I fully expect you will, then you will pay me five thousand pounds.'

This was a wholly unexpected complication but I was so taken aback by the complete set of rules that I hardly knew what to say. I just nodded in dazed agreement. Next they directed me to the sheet of paper that had the heading:

'A list of countries and towns to be visited whilst Walking round the World.'

This was an eye-catching itinerary, being first a very long and extensive traverse across the whole British Isles before crossing the Atlantic and following the western seaboard of North and South America, from there across to Australia and New Zealand, thence to South Africa, before heading back east to Asia and India, then through Egypt and Suez to Western Europe before finally arriving home. I will admit to being no cartographer but it seemed an eccentric journey.

'In order to ensure your safe conduct from country to country our lawyer has approached the Foreign Office for a document stating your intent and requesting free passage. We will also contact the various embassies and consulates en route so that they will be ready to assist you in any way possible.'

I had a thought, 'This assistant that you are employing, can he aid my journey in anyway?'

'What aid could he be, Harry?'

'It is already agreed that I will have to finance the trip out of the souvenirs that I sell. If the assistant could undertake the transactions then I could continue with the walking without interruption. In effect I would be the exhibit and he could be the box office.'

'That would be acceptable to us.'

'Good, then I can see a purpose for him.'

'Then if we all agree, we should sign.'

I took one of the fountain pens on the table, tested it on the blotting paper and signed with as much bravado as I could muster. The Earl and JP Morgan signed with a lot more diligence. The Earl then remarked, 'It goes without saying that none of the parties will mention the names of the others until this wager is complete or the task is forfeit.'

I sat back relieved. 'On January the first at ten thirty a.m. I will be ready to start the walk with your assistant in Trafalgar Square. I hope your man is ready.'

With that, I picked up my papers and left.

I travelled back to my family home in the country and made it known that I had met a fellow in London who offered me a position in an Importers and Exporters business in New Zealand. I'd once met a gentleman in this trade while sharing tips and bets during an afternoon at the races. Fortunately, I had gleaned enough knowledge of the exports of New Zealand to satisfy the inevitable probing questions from my father. As to what we were importing, spirits such as whisky and gin seemed the obvious answer.

While I was at home I begged to have the helmet from one of the suits of armour as a memento. I said I would have it on display in the office in New Zealand as a reminder of home. They did think it rather odd but finally relented. I had pangs of regret for the suit of armour that I took it from as it stood forlorn and headless in the long hall.

The perambulator was a much more difficult item to procure especially as I wanted to have the carriage painted with the purpose of the journey in the form of an advertisement. Obviously the purchase was easy but I needed to ensure that there was no trail back to me once a sign-writer had completed the transformation otherwise I should be quickly unmasked. I asked the Earl to help me. I took an alias and went to see one of his employees. This employee then went to see a theatrical costumier claiming to be in the process of buying props for a production that the Earl was partially funding. He asked if they could find a theatrical sign-writer to make a prop for a show. The perambulator was sent from the manufacturers to the sign-writer, who painted the perambulator. On the front he put the words 'A £21,000 wager' and on the sides he wrote, 'Walking round the World'. It was collected by the employee and he delivered the item to a photographer. I arrived incognito and a photograph was taken of me in the helmet with the perambulator. Numerous copies were made and delivered back to the Earl's employee. He then arranged for it to all be sent to my lock-up. That way, even if anybody realised that these goods were for the man in the mask, they would not have any route back to me.

The third item to get in order was myself. I was no athlete, having never walked further than to and from my club and even then only if the weather was pleasant or a hansom cab was not within hailing distance. I knew I had to change and indeed I wanted to, so I spent the last few months in preparation for the task ahead. I would walk to the outskirts of London and then take a train back to the capital. I started off walking as far as Mitcham, then as my boots wore in and my feet complained less I could reach Epsom. By Christmas time I was walking to Leatherhead before dusk set in. I was ready.

Challenge

London, New Year's Day, 1908

'For the first time since leaving home I did not go out to celebrate on New Year's Eve. I tried to sleep although the thoughts of the momentous change that was about to happen to my life made me toss and turn all night and my sleeping arrangements were far from usual. I had made a bed in my lock-up so that I would not be seen starting the venture by anyone who might recognise me. It was uncomfortably cold and I was glad to wake and make myself some breakfast. Fortunately there was a gas connection and I was able to brew some tea. The assistant arrived just after dawn. He was a few years younger than I, taller with dark hair, his face was pleasantly freckled and split by a lush moustache. He had the air of a man in excellent health. He introduced himself as Mr. Allen. I told him that I must assume a false name, so that he can address me in public and as I was walking with a knight's helmet upon my head we agreed that I be named after my favourite knight of the round table, Sir Lancelot. Mr. Allen required no alias but he told me that at school he had been known as 'Raider' after a notorious American Confederate bushwhacker named Quantrill, to whom he was distantly related. In this way we would prevent accidentally revealing my identity while on the road. On hearing about his notorious relative of whom he seemed enormously proud, I suggested he might try to speak with an American accent, just to add some glamour to the proceedings. He was good at imitating and already knew some American words and phrases like "Boy this is one lollapalooza" which he said he could use as thanks when people gave us money and "let's skidoo, kiddo" for when we needed to be moving on.

I collected together the items of clothing that had been set out in the conditions and these were placed with Raider's belongings in the perambulator. To the top of the helmet I had attached a sign of my own preparation that read 'Walking Round the World'. I made sure it was secure and then carefully began to place the helmet on my head. The interior of the helmet had a crisp metallic smell that took me back to my childhood. In my mind's eye I saw myself running along the long hall, chased by my brother. The reverie was broken when I became aware that the helmet was a tighter fit than I remembered. For the first time I fully experienced the physical closeness of the visor, hemming me in and at the same time shielding me from the outside world.

It was a dull and misty morning as we left the lock-up for the last time and hailed a hansom cab. The first cab that came was not big enough to carry the two of us and the perambulator, we needed a second, which fortunately for a New Year's Day morning, arrived rapidly. We disembarked at Charing Cross Station, paid the cab drivers, gathered our belongings and began the walk to Trafalgar Square.

Our arrival created an enormous amount of interest, much more than I could ever have imagined. Waiting in the square was a reporter from the Times who asked us a series of questions about our task and there was a photographer as well to document the start. Big Ben rang the half hour at ten thirty and as the conditions stipulated we began our long march. I don't think it is any exaggeration to say that we were mobbed. It seemed that everybody in Trafalgar Square wanted to get as close as possible. There were noisy cheering crowds alongside us every step of the way. Neither Raider nor I could sell our cards and pamphlets fast enough. That first day was extraordinary.

In the evening I discovered the first of many hardships. I could not eat nor drink without removing my helmet. I had allowed myself to imagine that once we had found accommodation of an evening I would be able to change and go out without being discovered but it was soon apparent that there were many flaws in such a plan. The clamour and interest from the public was enormous so I was forced to eat in my room, both dinner and breakfast. Raider would only open the door when I had the helmet on, otherwise the door had to be locked lest someone attempted to enter. Worse still I had to wear the helmet when going to and from the toilet.

The next day a dreadful thing happened that nearly ended the whole enterprise. We had just left our lodging in Bexleyheath when a young lad ran up and offered me a silver sixpence for a postcard. Without thinking I accepted it and a policeman who was standing nearby asked me if I had a pedlar's license. It was Raider who was named on the license, I was not supposed to take money so I tried to bluff my way through. The policeman would have none of it and arrested me. Fortunately, we just had to pay a fine and were let on our way without hindrance but for a short time this was most alarming.

From here on things rapidly fell into a routine. We would walk the roads, in amongst the horses and carts, horse-drawn buses and the occasional smelly motor rattletraps until we came to the outskirts of a town. Our appearance would immediately provoke the attention of children who would chase us up and down the street and within a very short time the world and his wife were aware of our imminent arrival. By the time we had made it to the High Street sometimes even the local dignitaries would already be there to greet us, as if we were doing their town a great honour by passing through it. We would stop for a while, listen to the hastily prepared speeches and then I might be asked to say a few words in response. I would thank them for their generous hospitality and say that it was only due to their kindness and continued support that this challenge could be completed and every single person there could take some credit for the eventual success of this expedition. I quickly learnt that the more credit you gave to the audience the more souvenirs were sold. Afterwards we would collect whatever paperwork Mr. Allen felt was necessary to document our passage and this would be placed in an envelope and sent to the PO Box that we had agreed for the journey.

I cannot stress enough just how much the days were long and challenging, we would try to walk about twelve miles, which doesn't sound far but the perambulator was heavy and not easy to negotiate along the rutted roads. Stopping and talking to people took its time as well. Then there were the simple tasks of daily life, finding a place to eat, to sleep, to wash and freshen up. After this came the important tasks of ensuring a ready supply of photographs and pamphlets and finally depositing the extra money in the bank. To say that the challenge quickly lost its glamour would be very true but my commitment was total and my resolve strengthened every day. The same could not be said of my assistant Mr. Allen. We were on the road up to North Devon from Cornwall at the time when he said he had walked far enough, he knew there was a railway station in the town and he was determined to go back to his previous life. It was just after three months he threw in the towel, making it plain that this task was far greater than he had imagined. He had a sweetheart and he missed her dearly and even though I was led to believe he was liable to make a substantial sum of money on completion, he handed me back his satchel and called it a day.

This meant a longer than normal stay in Barnstaple. I sent a message via the PO Box that Mr. Allen had left, requesting instructions as to how they would want me to proceed. After several days, the Earl sent me a letter through an intermediary, saying that a lad had been found to accompany me. He was a strapping youth, strong as an ox and full of spirit but a mere sixteen years old. However he rapidly took the mantle of assistant and was a very quick learner.

We walked on, county after county ticking off the places as we went. Where the original itinerary had us going backwards and forwards across the country we smoothed out the journey to make the most advantage from our labours.

We arrived in Newmarket around the time of the Cambridgeshire handicap. As it happened the King was attending the races and so it was that we were introduced to His Majesty Edward the VII. He was most entertained by my story and bought a postcard from me for five pounds, Royal patronage indeed. He asked me to sign it for him but I was so much in awe of His Majesty that I was unable to think of a way around it without revealing my identity, so I am afraid I was very rude and refused. I deeply regret that I did not sign it 'the man in the mask' but that thought came to me much later.

Months passed and finally we crossed the sea to Belfast, taking the steamer from Stranraer. The crowds were smaller in Ireland but we were still able to bank money. I could see that the ocean journeys ahead would be very expensive and had long practised thrift on the road. The old me, the West End playboy would have casually frittered away the cash but I had a new goal now and anyway there was little I could spend money on, as an overabundance of food or drink just made the next day's travels more difficult.

Assistants, they arrived with happy dispositions but the journey quickly broke their stamina and spirit. A frequent task was finding someone to complete the next leg, because it was easier to employ someone for three months than an unspecified time with no guarantee of when it might end.

The walk through Ireland was much more straightforward. From Belfast, through Dublin and finally to Cork to board one of the steamships colloquially known as an Atlantic greyhound which would take us on to Quebec. We continued to send back reports of our progress and before our arrival in the port of Cork I received a message saying that we should book our passage on the White Star Line, as arrangements had been made to allow us safe passage to Canada. Travelling between Scotland and Ireland was easy as there was no great necessity to prove my identity. The challenge was still well known amongst the public and therefore there was no problem in boarding the steamer. Travel to a new continent was a different matter. Some form of identification and purpose of travel was a significant requirement. However the Earl and JP Morgan had remarkable influence and provided me with letters of introduction from the British Foreign Office and several important bodies including the Embassies of America and other important countries along the route.

I forget the details of the actual liner but it had set sail from Liverpool on its way to Quebec. We were expected by the steamship company when we arrived in the port. My assistant was not willing to travel to Canada and I said goodbye to him at the dockside. I had booked an inside cabin but the White Star Line wanted to upgrade me to an outside view. I said that I could not in all honesty take this gift as I required the extra privacy. Despite my protestations, my cabin was upgraded to one with a much more luxurious suite with its own bathroom. As was my custom, I took all my meals in my room and sometimes members of the crew would come to visit me. They treated me very well despite my hermit-like existence.

This was my first taste of long distance travel and I found myself with plenty of time on my hands. The boat had a fine library and they were able to furnish me with maps of the world and information about other steamship routes between the continents. I spent a long time playing with different possibilities and soon a plan emerged. I desired to make the route more manageable as I realised the conditions did not set out exactly when I should or should not walk, they just spelt out the order in which the countries should be approached. It was rule fifteen that really set me thinking.

"To be allowed to go as you please."

If I could go as I pleased then it pleased me to use steamships. I looked at my savings account and it was in rude health. I wouldn't always be able to travel first class but I could definitely afford the travel. I would still walk of course but there were places on the itinerary that might be far more challenging than the British Isles. South America for example could be much more easily negotiated as a series of shipping stops.

Arrival in Quebec was a simple, quiet affair. The purser helped me to take down my perambulator and introduced me to the immigration officer. After a short discussion about who I was and why I was wearing such alarming attire he looked through my papers and then required me to accompany him to his office. Once inside he asked me to take off my helmet, not so that he may recognise me but to allow him to check that I did not meet the description of any felons who were at large. I asked him to assure me that this was no trick and he was not attempting to unmask me. I made him promise that he would not reveal my identity nor would he describe me to anyone. He went further and said as long as he was satisfied that I was not evading justice then he would not discuss any part of this episode with anyone.

I did not want to do this as it could jeopardise the whole task but I could see that I would not be allowed to enter Canada if I did not comply with his request. I looked this man over, he was an upright and moral fellow who would brook no nonsense. I asked him if he would lock the door. He did so and for the first time since New Year's Eve two years previously, someone other than one of my assistants gazed upon my face. My beard had grown wildly as the visor did allow some of my face to be seen and I felt this would give me extra protection against discovery. My hair was in a terrible state because I had not seen a barber in all of this time. In order to keep it from being too unruly I had requested that my assistants cut my hair but they knew as much about barbering as I do about shearing sheep and their efforts were mainly for comfort rather than look. Although my appearance alarmed him, the officer was quickly assured that there was no one of my likeness trying to flee justice. I also felt some connection between us. Maybe my face betrayed the enormity of the challenge that I was undertaking and he treated me with utmost respect, helping me to the port gates and pointing out some landmarks for me to follow.

The walking itself was not a concern. I would rise early, take breakfast in my room if possible and then prepare for the day's journey. I would collect my clothes from the drying room and place all my items in the perambulator, then check the tyres for wear, oil the wheels because they would bind up, especially in the snow. Finally, I would consult my maps and make note of the towns and villages on my route for the day and then set off. Canada in winter was bitterly cold and required many more layers of clothing. I could not walk very far each day but I reasoned that any distance was better than none. I was walking south but slowly and beginning to realise that weather in the Americas is much more extreme than in England.

Confusingly, each place I travelled through had its own rules and regulations regarding the sale of goods. My innocent souvenirs, the primary source of income were in fact a liability that could bring me into conflict with the law. This was a risk too great to bear so reluctantly I stopped selling the postcards and pamphlets to prevent such a calamity. I looked at the funds that had been amassed from our British benefactors and reasoned that if I were to continue the journey alone without an assistant, it would be possible for me to complete it without further income.

In the British Isles everywhere we went we were met with great acclaim and enthusiasm. I was a person of note and much in demand but once abroad I held very little glamour for the people. At best I was an English eccentric gentleman, at worst an itinerant vagabond. My comings and goings were of little interest and my travels no longer brought out the great and good to see me. Only the dogs marked my passing with a loud chorus of suspicious barks.

I had the perambulator repainted so as to obliterate its advertised claims and I investigated other headgear, hats and scarves and such-like, so I would no longer make such a spectacle of myself, the risk of being recognised now being much reduced.

The days turned into weeks and ground was covered, the itinerary took me down the eastern seaboard and eventually to New Orleans. From here I took a steamer down to Rio and another on to Montevideo. I collected my stamp and crossed on the ferry to Buenos Aires and it was here that I used condition fifteen more liberally still. Argentina is a fine country with an excellent rail network. The walk to Santiago in Chile would have been long, arduous and unprofitable while a sea trip through the Straits of Magellan was still regarded as hazardous. Instead I booked a train journey of some magnitude but it did not go all the way as the Andes are a remarkable barrier. I still had a considerable climb to undertake on old Inca paths but it saved me much time, allowing me to cross the Southern Continent of the Americas in weeks rather than months.

From here on I used boats and trains liberally, that is not to say I did not walk, I certainly did, miles and miles every day, making sure that I visited a cobbler whenever I recognised one. I can say that I've bought shoe leather in every currency imaginable.

My itinerary would suggest that I saw the world. The facts are that I physically went around the world but the terms of the wager were a barrier to allowing me the freedom to enjoy the places that I travelled through. I felt the sun through my headgear, I experienced the cold in every bone of my body, I knew fatigue, I slept in beds of every type and ate food from the most grey and insipid to the fiery curries of India. I was ill with cold, with sickness, with headaches but most of the time I was fit and well. However I saw very little of the world and met very few people beyond the curious. Even when I stayed in a city for a few days regaining my strength I never felt I belonged there, because I always knew I would be moving on.

Six years and eight months into the challenge saw me disembarking from a boat that had left Alexandria in Egypt four days earlier for Genoa. There was no one to meet me and very little interest in a man with a perambulator. However there had been much fevered speculation on the boat amongst the other passengers about recent events in Europe. The Austro-Hungarian Empire had declared war upon Serbia leading the Russians to mobilise on behalf of its ally, which in turn stirred up German retaliation. Somehow Britain was becoming embroiled in this, as Germany was threatening to invade Belgium and apparently Britain had given Germany an ultimatum that Belgium must remain neutral.

There was much heat amongst the conversation of the various nationalities on the boat. I had spent the voyage in my cabin but I often overheard snatches of worrying gossip. The first thing I needed to do on disembarking was find out what was actually happening in the world, before that I had to submit myself to the indignities of the border police. The process was essentially the same every time I entered into a new country. I would offer my bona fides, the paperwork from the foreign office and the London embassy of the nation I was entering explaining my mission and why it was important that my anonymity be protected. Then I would ask to be taken to a room because I had found there was no reasonable argument to their request to ensure that I was not a wanted fugitive. I had to show them my face and sometimes submit to a photograph being taken that could be sent to my proposed route of departure to ensure that I was indeed leaving the country.

On this occasion it was significantly different because it was I that eagerly asked the questions. The officer was a kindly old gentleman who spoke passable English. He requested that I remove the helmet and once I had done so I implored him to tell me what was happening in Europe. He shook his head and said it was all madness and then with a mirthless laugh added that what no one can believe is that Britain had declared war on Germany to defend the honour and freedom of Belgium, in his opinion, a remarkable act of folly. Already Germany and the Austro-Hungarian Empire were fighting Russia and France. He was glad that Italy was remaining neutral and staying out of the stupidity of war.

I was utterly stunned at this moment. Being away from home for so long had caused me to forget the power struggles of empires and nations but here it was, the very countries that I proposed to walk through were now deadly enemies. I sat in silence and let this news sink in. It was the end of everything, six years and eight months of travelling nearly thirty thousand miles and now with about seven thousand miles left to walk that would take maybe two or three years to complete, the wager was over. Events had conspired to deny me the prize. Despite all my efforts the task could not be completed.

My silence and demeanour caused concern to the Officer who helped me sit down while he found me some water to drink. Some moments later I accepted the refreshment gladly and then stood up.

I had made my mind up, I told him, I would be leaving on the next available boat to Britain.

As it happened, it took me nearly a month to get back home to Southampton. The docks were being refitted to allow soldiers to embark for the front in France. I hastened to London and a fateful meeting with the Earl in his club beside Covent Garden Market. It was late afternoon and the costermongers and flower sellers were packing away after a busy day. It seemed incongruous to see flowers at a time of war but they were still doing a brisk trade. I asked the doorman of the club to send a message to the Earl's residence notifying him of my arrival and that I needed to talk with him urgently.

The bar of his club was as quiet as a church with only the older members inhabiting the chairs. In contrast the Earl entered the room with the energy of a troupe of horses. He came right up to me and drank me in. Finally he said, 'How extraordinary, out of the blue you just appear!'

'Indeed I do,' I replied. 'Although I am sure you are up to date with my travels, I've certainly kept you well informed. However a month ago I arrived in Genoa to begin the European leg of the journey which would complete the wager to find the world turned upside down.'

'In Genoa, you say?'

'Indeed and if I may remind you from there I would have had to walk through France, Belgium, Germany and Holland. I have faced many enemies on my travels but I think that an armed one would be an inconvenience too far, so I have temporarily ceased the walk. My country's need is greater than any wager. I intend to join the Army and do my duty for King and Country. God willing, once peace returns I will be able to continue.'

'I will send a telegram to JP this evening and make him aware of your reappearance. Last I heard he was in Rome. This war has changed everything. You are lucky to catch me here because I'm due to return to Cumberland. The Army has asked me to form this thing that they call 'a Pals Battalion,' no good for you I suppose? Your pals, such as they are, aren't from Cumberland?'

'I've already made arrangements.'

'Good luck Harry, I hope you have a good war.'

That was the last time I saw him. He shook my hand and left with a look of utter bemusement. Meanwhile I joined a local regiment and after a period of training was sent out to France but before I left I received a letter from the Earl saying the wager had been called off due to the war.

Things did not go well for me in France. I was not a natural soldier and I was unlucky to be twice hit by shrapnel. On the second occasion I was invalided out of the Army and that was after only a year of service. So I came home and tried to do what I could for the country by joining the recruitment campaign, to inspire the more able-bodied to follow my example and fight in the war. Due to this I was often away from home at the Hall, so what happened next was a devastating blow. My father had a portfolio of investments that were the base rock of the family income but he had unwisely become involved in Russian Bonds. Then came the revolution and almost overnight we were penniless. The shocking change of our family's circumstances was too much for my father, his heart failed him and he died a pauper, buried in an unmarked grave. My mother, heartbroken and destitute, fell terribly low and within weeks she had joined him in the cemetery. At the same time my elder brother was killed at the front. Truly this was a tragedy for the whole family.

It was touch and go for me at that time but somehow I found the strength to continue. With my military bearing I found simple work as a cinema doorman and slowly I got back on my feet. From there on I have lived a small, quiet life with my wife and my children. They are my touchstones now. So that's been my life. The walk redeemed me. I may not have completed the challenge, I did not win the wager but I found a prize beyond money because it gave me purpose, meaning and the gifts to survive the calamities that followed.'

Chance

Doncaster, Easter 1977

TAPE 2 – SIDE 1

Dad said, 'That was the story he told and the one you see in all the papers. It wasn't the whole story though.'

'Why not Dad, what was wrong with it?' asked Gillian.

'He hadn't mentioned a word about my mother, not one word, so I challenged him and he looked a little sheepish, probably hoping that I wasn't listening out for news on her. It was the end of visiting time and Matron had rung the ward bell and was asking people to leave saying that the patients need their rest. Some white-coated young doctor came in and wanted to take a look at Harry so I made to leave and as I did so he said, 'Are you coming back tomorrow?' I said I was, though I hadn't planned to, in fact I needed to get back home but he said he would have an answer for me tomorrow. I said it might have to be the weekend because I needed to check with work that they could give me more time off and he said he wasn't going anywhere. I left and I didn't get back until Sunday.

It was a mucky drab day when I made my way back to the hospital in Brighton. Harry was still there, he was sitting up in bed but he didn't look so clever. The pack of cards were scattered all over the bed. I was amazed the Matron hadn't got him to tidy it up as she liked to keep the ward shipshape and Harry looked anything but that day. He brightened up when he saw me coming and cracked a bit of a smile. He was glad to see me and said he had been waiting for my visit because he had something to tell me, something he had never told anyone else. Then he started speaking in a low whisper.

'I was a different man then and I have changed but I regret to say I did not treat your mother well.'

I anxiously replied, 'I still want to hear it. I have waited all my life to hear the truth.'

'I told you I was a bit of a man about town, I loved to go to dances and other gentlemanly pursuits. That was not even the half of it really. I loved to drink and get merry with my friends, I enjoyed the company of women, many women, especially at the various dances throughout the season.'

'I went to the dance that fateful evening after a disastrous day at Ascot. It was a bad day at the end of a worse week and the culmination of a truly appalling year. My allowance was running dry and I did not need the services of a fortune teller to foresee that a very unhappy meeting with my father was imminent.

At the ball in the Dorchester I bumped into two older gentlemen, one of whom I recognised as the Earl. We fell into conversation and the good news was that they were going to have a card game that evening and they were looking for people to make up the numbers for a table at the Sportsman's club. On my way I touched as many of my pals as I could to raise some cash to see me through the game. When I arrived a steward led me to one of the smaller rooms where cards could be played in relative privacy. I was surprised to find that only the Earl and JP Morgan were seated. We were to be three. Despite the small numbers it was all very convivial. The Earl called for some brandy and soda and we played.

The first few hands went by and nothing much happened, they chatted idly about a strange idea of walking round the world but it was only gentlemanly talk. Then as often happens it looked as though the cards were changing or at least there was some value to them but it never went my way. I was not losing big, just watching my pot slowly dwindle as the Earl persistently won. My experience of his type of player had taught me that he was more likely to be reckless after a good hand. Then he won a substantial pot from JP and was becoming more expansive with his cards. JP meanwhile was harder to read but so far had not tried anything flashy. It was at this moment that I was dealt this perfect hand, an absolute gem on any given day, a full house king high and I knew this was the time to get my year back on track. All I needed to do was fill the pot and land this hand of cards and then I could avoid the grovelling meeting with father and get myself ahead of the game for the rest of the year.

When you have a good hand what you don't want is for the other players to drop out too soon. You need the pot to go deep but I didn't have the resources to take it all the way. The cards in my hand were crying out for my backing, so what was there to do? The good news was that the Earl and JP were obviously happy with their hands and the pot was bidding up. The pot had reached nearly a thousand pounds and I had no further money that I could raise. JP bid it up further and the Earl folded. I could not afford to fold but I could not afford to see him either, I was in a bind and there was only one thing to do. It was time for the biggest gamble of my life when I said I would put my entire inheritance against the pot. JP was aghast and asked if I was absolutely sure but the Earl was highly amused and rested back in his seat as if enjoying a particularly bloody ringside spectacle. 'I'm out,' he said. 'It's between you and Harry.'

'I will see you, Harry.'

The cards were turned, I lay my full house down with a flourish only to be met with a straight flush. My fortune was no more. I had wagered and lost my inheritance to JP Morgan. I was utterly ruined.

Etiquette would say that I would be led out of the club and left to wander about as either a pauper having signed off my inheritance or as a social pariah having welched on a gambling debt. I knew my father would not pay up, even if I had signed over my inheritance, so the most likely outcome would be confinement to a miserable existence on my father's estate with my affairs tightly constrained.

So how would it be possible to avoid such a fate? It was then that the strange conversation earlier came back to me. I was ready to clutch at the most broken of straws.

'What if you could offer me an alternative forfeit?'

The Earl replied, 'It is not our intention to ruin you but what forfeit could possibly interest us.'

'What about the journey around the World?'

The Earl was dismissive. 'What of it Harry?'

'What if I undertake to make a never before attempted record and if I achieve it then you will write off my debt but if I don't then you take everything.'

J.P. joined in the conversation. 'I am reluctant to take all of your worldly goods Harry but at the same time I am not inclined to let you off the hook.'

'Neither am I. If we agree to this idea of yours, you can expect that we will impose some very rigorous terms and in no way will we finance any aspect of it, you must fund this escapade yourself.'

I replied. 'Right here, right now I am a ruined man and I am willing to agree to any and all of your conditions. Please set out your terms.'

The Earl finished the conversation, 'We will meet here at my club in London in a week and let you know our decision.'

So that was the last time I gambled but what a wager, to walk round the world or my life as I knew it was over, because to renege on my word would have meant being ostracised by my friends and my club. I would have to return home and become a recluse. It was obvious to me that they did not believe that I would even start the challenge but I did.

It was a few weeks later that I met your mother. She was an attractive woman and walking along the way we just took easily to each other. It's difficult to believe that one thing led to another, because how can a man in a mask woo a woman? Despite, or maybe because of the extraordinary circumstances romance did bloom. You say you are Jim Beasley, that was the surname that I used as an alias with your mother, lest anyone should attempt to uncover my identity, which was a frequent risk.

We didn't have a huge stock of postcards and part of the routine was to find a local photographer and get postcards made. For a while your mother appeared with us as we made our way round Britain and that's how she found her way onto those post cards. I am surprised that you still have a copy though. They sold in their thousands. There never seemed to be any left at the end of the day.

For a few months your mother came along the route. She became Mrs Iron Mask and for a while we were happy but the magic wore thin. Life on the road was not easy and the weather became changeable. It was all very trying for your mother, because she had become pregnant with you. It was asking a lot of her so she went back to her home and had you and I sent her money when I could. Once I had left Britain I became acutely aware of my precarious pecuniary position and I needed all the money I had to complete the challenge, so I stopped sending anything back to your mother and to my shame I made no effort to contact her again.

I carried on with the challenge, on and on until arriving in Genoa that fateful August in 1914. With Europe descending into war, any hope of completing the wager and escaping my fate was dashed. I rapidly came back to Britain and sought out the Earl. He was busy with preparations of his own but he had a little time to tell me some remarkable news. In the card game that changed my life, if you remember, I actually lost to JP Morgan. He was to receive all the winnings should I fail in my quest but he had died a few months earlier and in his will he had explicitly cancelled this outstanding gambling debt.

I was free of my obligation at last. It was over and I could come home and start my life again. However I still felt I owed a debt, so I joined the Army to do my bit in the war. The walking, then the war, it had changed me. As I already told you I was invalided out of the army and when the family lost their fortune, I was the only one of all of us who had learnt how to survive on small amounts of money.

There is one further matter I have not been candid about. I was already married before this all began, we were very young and the marriage did not go well and we had parted. When these calamities befell my family in 1917 my first wife found me and we found that we had both changed. Together we decided to give the marriage a second chance. It was not easy but my mind was made up to make a small success out of the rest of my life and that was what happened.

I want to say that I am not a bad man, although I have made bad choices and I have been swayed by wine, women and gambling. More to the point I was never good at being a good man but the only time in my life when I did my best was when I wore the mask.'

That was it, that was the end of his extraordinary tale and the last time I saw your grandfather as he died a few days later at home.

END OF RECORDING

PART 2

Begin at the beginning

Harry

Thetford, August 4, 1890

It's freezing. Oh, my fingers breathe on them quick. It's so chilly now that the moon has set, though when it shone earlier it seemed to take the warmth out of me with its cold white light. I can hear the sheep though. No, don't think about them you'll waken yourself, I don't want to waken but why can't I get to sleep? I just want to close my eyelids and drift off.

Pa told me to keep my eyes peeled so I'd better take notice, I look up at the stars and make patterns of sheep because there's nothing else to think about. I'm calling those stars over to the West the Great Ewe with its massive tail though I've never seen a sheep with a tail that's as long as its body. I reckon that Aries the Ram must be somewhere in the sky but they don't teach you things like that in the schoolhouse. For proper knowledge you need to get told it by someone who knows. They teach you to read and write though. Pa can't see the bother of it because it cost him a shilling a week that he said he could make better use of in the Red Lion.

'I can't read and write,' he always says, 'and I never had no harm'.

I bought a newspaper once because I liked to take a look at the words and he laughed at me, 'What's the point of that, boy,' he says, 'you can't wear it or eat it or drink it? It has no use.'

Though I say, 'It's not true, it's got use because you can know about things.'

'Like what?' He says.

'Look at this picture, it's a bridge in Scotland that has just opened. You can take a steam train to Aberdeen.'

'What do I want to do that for boy? I don't know no Scotch men.'

'Well, take a see at this article about market day, it tells the price of sheep,' I say, 'it's all here in the paper about what took place last Friday.'

'So what,' he says, 'if I want to know the price of sheep I'll ask a farmer. Them's the boys that know.'

'Yes but Old Hubbard told me that he sees the prices in the paper and they've been going the right way so now is the time for him to go to market and that's all because he reads the paper.'

Then Pa screws up my newspaper and puts it in the hearth. Quick as, he gives me a clip with the back of his hand and as far as he cares that's the talking over.

What's that? What's that black thing moving? It's only a crow hopping down the field. Sheep must have disturbed it. What's it doing on the ground? Crazy crow, you should be asleep in the trees.

I've never known it so cold and it's only August but I suppose I've never been out all night. My scarf's all damp, jacket's all damp, legs are all soggy and there is no sign of the dawn, not even a glimmering on the horizon.

Sheep are all here? Yes, they stay nearby because they're not so dumb whatever people might think. Try and get a hold of one if you think they are, they soon catch on to your thoughts.

Still, it beats being at home out here on the slope. I've got a choice of where I can lie down and don't have no grumbling brothers kicking and pushing me. Think I will get up and have a look see at what's what round the park. Seems a bit lighter over to the East and some of the sheep are on their feet too.

If I was indoors I wouldn't feel the cold so sharp, cut to the marrow. Why didn't they tell me it would be so nippy? I'd have cadged my brother's big jacket when he wasn't looking. He doesn't need it at night anyhow.

I've never been out all of the night before and I wouldn't be here at all if it weren't for old Tovey falling over a ditch and breaking his leg. They took him to the sawbones up by the Post Office and he yelled and yelled. The whole town heard him and I fancy I can still hear his cries up here on the top field, in with the rustling leaves, hooting owls and the lonesome bark of the dogs from the town.

The sky is reddening to the East, shepherd's warning so they say. I suppose I'm a shepherd now. What's my warning I wonder and where did I put my sack and my stick? Come on sheep, raise yourselves, we're moving on down. What about a bit of a sing-song, the 'Norfolk Turnip' to give us some zip?

> *Some counties vaunt themselves in pies*
> *and some in meat excel.*
> *For turnips of enormous size*
> *fair Norfolk bears the belle,*
> *fair Norfolk bears the belle.*

Move along now sheep, move along, you've got a place to be this morning. Old Hubbard's going to make his fortune and I'll see a shilling or two.

> *At midnight hour a hardy Knight*
> *was riding o'er the ley.*
> *The stars and moon had lost their light,*
> *and he had lost his way.*

What's a ley? I've never heard nothing of a ley before except in this ditty. Come on you stragglers, leave that grass, there's better to be had in the next field.

> *In vain he sought full half the night.*
> *No shelter could he spy.*
> *Pity it were so bold a Knight*
> *ill-served of cold should die.*

Another night of cold and I will perish too, let alone some blasted knight. Move aside sheep, let me see to the gate. Well, look at that sight down in the next hollow, all them haystacks in a white sea. That mist looks eerie, I'll lose my sheep in that if I don't take care.

> *When from a hollow turnip near*
> *there came a sudden light.*
> *A friendly voice with accent clear*
> *did thus address the Knight.*

Look over there, that's funny, funny peculiar, there's a light come on over by the big hall. A door opened and let someone out. Reckon it's a bit early for the gardeners but comforting to think I'm not alone out here.

> *Sir Knight, no demon dwelleth here.*
> *No giant keeps this house*
> *but tway poor drovers, goodman Vere,*
> *and honest Robin Rouse.*

It's a girl, look at that, who is she? That long brown hair isn't familiar and she definitely wasn't at the school house. I had better look away because I don't want her thinking I'm staring.

> *We twayne have taken shelter here*
> *with oxen, ninety-two*
> *and if you'll enter, never fear,*
> *there's room enough for you!*

She's pretty though and she's got the right idea, gathering kindling. When I get to the bottom of Hubbard's field, I'll make a fire and warm myself up. Now there's a plan, thank you, young lady, I'll sing up good and loud.

> *Some counties vaunt themselves in pies*
> *and some in meat excel.*
> *For turnips of enormous size*
> *fair Norfolk bears the belle,*
> *fair Norfolk bears the belle...*

Kate

On a metal framed bed in a room with bare boards, a shy young girl with long auburn hair and warm brown eyes sits with her head full of wonder. Her body is taut and her mind is anxious as her eyes explore the room. Her thin hands drift across the woollen blanket, caress the crisp white sheet and investigate the unusually plump softness of the feather pillow. She stands up and peeks cautiously inside the brown wooden wardrobe beside the bed, in which she glimpses half a dozen or so black dresses on hangers with matching white pinnies. Her first impression is that these are several sizes too big for her slight physique.

The butler, an imposing presence who had escorted her in a stately manner to this room, had first guided her around the hall. Along the main corridor they walked past suits of armour gleaming in the late afternoon sun and the girl had shaken her head at these marvels.

Then she had been led through the downstairs rooms filled with plush furniture, deep carpets and rich curtains and the butler had pointed out various items, the most startling of which were the huge paintings that hung on the walls. Portraits of the grand nobility with horses, swords and hunting dogs. Along with pretty ladies in old fashioned dresses amongst sylvan landscapes, their likenesses fading slowly away underneath the grimy deposits of smoke from the fires in the hall.

After walking through to the servants' areas, the laundry, the parlour and the noise and bustle of the kitchen, they returned to the main corridor where the butler opened a small door hidden in a wood panel. This revealed a higgledy piggledy staircase that seemed to snake around the whole house before arriving at the top floor. Here he led her to this room where she is now sitting, her mind filling with mounting disbelief.

She stands and moves towards the window, a few short steps because this is not a large room. If she were taller she would be forced to bend as the gable slopes abruptly but there is no need for her to crouch to enjoy the view. Below she can see a garden with walls around it, beyond that a straggly copse of trees and then fields.

The girl turns to examine the most astonishing thing in the room. Beside the doorframe is a gleaming round brass switch and when the switch is pressed, an action that she has repeated several times, the bare bulb of an electric light shines harshly in the centre of the ceiling.

From the open door she can hear a distant bell chiming and something the butler said earlier comes back to her, 'The dinner bell. Come to the servants' hall when you hear it.' Quickly she slips into a dress and pinny, then hangs up her only possessions, the raggedy clothes that she was wearing in her brown wardrobe and with some regret she leaves the new found sanctuary of her bedroom.

The return journey down the back stairs is long and convoluted, especially for someone who has not yet grasped the geography of the house but she is ravenous and hunger leads her to the right place. The servants' hall is hot, filled with the smells of cooking and noisy as a large group of staff have gathered for their dinner.

At the head of the table is the familiar face of the butler. He catches the girl's eye and gestures that she should take an empty seat at the other end of the table. The butler then taps his plate, the servants quieten and take their seats and he says grace. Then he stands up and addresses the staff. 'You will have noticed we have a new member with us this evening. This is Kate Green, she starts here tomorrow as an in-between maid under the direction of myself and cook. Please make her welcome.'

Kate blushes and sits immobile as she feels the eyes of the rest of the servants fall upon her. Beside Kate sits the hall boy, his hands marked with boot polish. He is even smaller than Kate and quieter if that were possible and he mumbles a short welcome. The other staff at the table introduce themselves. The lady's maid acknowledges her with refined and elegant politeness. The cook smiles and welcomes her with a gentle easy manner, though her assistant the scullery maid is awkward and shy. The footman is aloof and makes no special welcome and she feels he has no time for in-between maids. Sitting nearby are the gardeners, who look weary and weathered as they make small signs of welcome.

Dinner is served and Kate accepts everything that she is offered and finding it much more palatable than food she had eaten before, quickly empties her plate to the amusement of the other staff. Finally the meal is over and she returns to her room to lie down on her bed and gaze straight at the light in the centre of the ceiling. Each time she closes her eyes she can still see the outline of its glowing filament shimmering on her retina. Her eyes moisten as Kate for the first time contemplates the events of the day. Here she is, so far from her birthplace and yet she feels safe.

There is a knock on the door. 'Lights out, Miss Green, goodnight.' She flicks the brass switch for the last time but sleep is elusive.

A second knock. 'Wake up, Miss Green, you are needed in the kitchen.' It is the cook's voice and Kate is astonished to discover that she has slept after all. Outside the dawn is still a distant promise, so Kate fumbles for the light switch and with a loud click the bulb emits its harsh light.

Downstairs in the kitchen, Cook stands over the work table weighing out flour with a large set of brass scales. Seeing Kate she says, 'Take this jug and draw me some water my love and clean your hands while you're there. We're going to make some dough.'

Kate takes the earthenware jug, walks nimbly across the cold flagstone floor and fills it with several large pushes on the hand pump. Kate then takes a bar of soap and a bowl and gives her hands a good scour. Cook meanwhile has warmed some milk and sugar in a pan and is now dissolving yeast into it. Almost immediately bubbles are rising to the surface.

'Have you ever made bread, my darling?'

Kate shakes her head.

'You're a quiet one, aren't you just? There's nothing wrong in that in fact some prefer it but you are going to have to speak up when you are helping me in the kitchen. So pass over that jug, I'm going to dabble some water in this here bowl with the flour and yeast. Then mix it all up and after all that we are going to knead it. I can see you don't know what that means so I'll show you.'

Cook combines the ingredients together with several pinches of salt and then dusts the surface of the marble table top with flour and empties the dough from her large bowl. It looks wet and sticky as cook plunges her hands into the centre of the floury mound and stretches and folds the dough.

'Kate isn't it? We'll do this together. Show me your hands, good they look clean enough. Now can you sing a song?'

Kate was not expecting that question and momentarily she was taken back to her previous life where singing in chapel was an ordeal, so she mumbles, 'No.'

'No? Well, young Kate, when you are kneading dough it takes time and effort and little sing-song makes the job go easy like. So I'm going to start us off with a hymn, a simple one and you just join in when you're ready.'

Cook passes some of the sticky dough over to Kate and together they push and turn and roll it while Cook sings 'All things bright and beautiful.' Soon Kate feels more embarrassed about not joining in with the singing and she is humming along too. After a few minutes and some handfuls of flour, the dough loses its stickiness and becomes soft and elastic. Cook stops kneading and rubs the last of the dough from her fingers. 'Enough, we'll let it rest now while we get the oven warmed and you have pretty voice, young Kate, when you choose to use it.'

'Thank you' says Kate, she blushes as she realises that she was singing along but Cook has brought a smile to her face with the compliment about her voice.

After breakfast, the butler fetches Kate from the kitchen and takes her around the drawing rooms on the ground floor. In each room she bends down at the grate and with a stiff brush sweeps away the remnants of the fire into an iron bucket. The ashes look grey and lifeless but the embers can suddenly glow with unexpected heat. It is dirty work but the butler explains that it is expected that the grates will be emptied each morning and the room will remain spotlessly clean as will her uniform, making it a slow and laborious task.

The butler takes Kate to meet the housekeeper who was not at the dinner table the night before as she lives outside the hall with her husband in a house in the town. A flinty middle-aged woman, she briskly supplies Kate with polish and dusters and leads her into a side drawing room where there is furniture to wipe and polish and pretty ornaments to dust and clean. Under the watchful gaze of the housekeeper and the portraits on the walls, Kate handles these objects with great care, recognising their fragility and respecting their value. Satisfied with Kate's progress the housekeeper shows her several more rooms and tells her that this will be part of her routine.

Back in the kitchen, Kate asks Cook what a routine is and Cook replies. 'It's something you do every day, except when you have a day off.' Kate nods but she is unsure if she has a day off.

As Kate works her way around the downstairs rooms she contemplates her new life here in the hall in Norfolk. Yesterday she was sitting in a carriage that bumped and rolled its way for nearly a day from the poor house in Ipswich and now to have regular food, to be clothed, to have a small amount of privacy, these are things that Kate has never taken for granted before. It becomes her opinion that providence has been kind to her at last.

Outside, the red brick of the hall soaks up the warming rays of the sun banishing the draughts and chills of winter. Soon there will be no need for a fire of an evening and the task of cleaning the grates will be over for the season. There will always be cooking, cleaning, dusting and polishing and Kate rises early and works hard each day.

May 11th

On Sunday morning the sun has already risen when Kate is woken. She comes down to the kitchen to find Cook making a large breakfast for all the servants and the talk is of dressing up in their best clothes because today they will be going to the church.

Cook asks her to help with preparing the roast for lunch. On the work table there stands a large wicker basket of herbs bejewelled with dewdrops that the gardeners harvested earlier. Cook turns the mixture out onto a wooden cutting board and taking a huge knife chops them finely. Then she peels the skin from a few cloves of garlic and deftly minces them. Now she throws some salt onto the board and rubs the herbs and garlic together making a fine paste.

'Take the beef, my love and lie it flat, meat side up.'

Kate takes the heavy, cold joints and tries to lay them flat on the marble table. The thick creamy fat on the bottom side makes the beef curl and Kate holds it down as best she can. Cook scoops up the fine herb paste in her hands and slathers it across the meat, working it into the folds and crevices. Then she slices some butter and places that on top. Quickly she takes the whole slab of beef and rolls it up, using some skewers to keep its shape and finally with some string she tightly ties each joint into a large roll.

'There you go, that's my little secret, all ready for the oven. They just need a few moments to rest and then they can cook.'

The kitchen range has been warming and Kate helps cook settle the huge joints of beef into the metal roasting trays. Cook gingerly opens the hot cast-iron doors and positions the meat carefully on the wire shelves. Turning to Kate she says. 'You and me, we are going to the church this morning' and then she instructs the scullery maid to keep a watchful eye on the meat and baste it every thirty minutes while she is away.

Kate is alarmed because unlike the other servants she does not have an outfit that could be described as Sunday best. Fortunately Cook has an answer. There is a store of leftover clothes that the laundry maid oversees from servants who have worked at the hall and have moved on for one reason or another. The clothes are not beautiful, most of them are tired and worn but they are better than the raggedy dress that she was given when she left the poor house, her own clothes being in such bad repair that they were destroyed when she was admitted.

Quickly she changed into a neat blue dress that was about her size and Cook even found her an old blue and black bonnet that gave the ensemble a respectable air. Together they strolled into the town and although Kate was not comfortable in her new clothes, she did not feel conspicuous.

The pebble and flint stone tower of St Cuthbert's church in the centre of Thetford was visible for a distance. At the main entrance under some trees, people were gathering to meet up and gossip. Cook bade good day to some of the townsfolk which did make Kate feel self-conscious as she was unsure what to say or do.

Inside the warmth of the late spring sun had not yet penetrated to the nave and the congregation shivered and rubbed their arms to encourage the circulation. As the church filled it seemed to slowly come alive and Kate was aware that she was witnessing something new.

The service began with a hymn and the congregation singing as a joyful whole, rather than the tuneless and discordant noise of the boys and girls in the poor house. Kate began to feel an inner warmth and this feeling deepened during the vicar's sermon. Here she heard things that were never said from the pulpit in the poor house chapel, where the themes either were wickedness and the road to hell, or obedience and respect as the path to forgiveness.

Here her past was all but forgotten, as the calm gentle voice of the vicar echoed softly in this old flint church. He spoke of peace and love and Kate found herself for the first time starting to realise that life, her life, could be very different.

After the morning service Cook heads straight back to the hall and Kate tags on behind. After changing back into her pinny she returns to the kitchen where the aroma of the roasting beef and its herbs and spices fills the room. Cook is moving the trays of roasting meat from one shelf to another in the oven. Kate is set to work peeling potatoes and scrubbing vegetables which Cook then slices and boils and roasts until it seems to Kate that there is more food being cooked at this moment than she has ever seen before. The clamour and rush comes to a crescendo and then order and peace is restored as the food is artfully arranged on the serving plates and dispatched to the main table in a procession of silver platters, escorted by the butler and the hall boy.

On their return the plates are stacked, the pudding is served and the servants can at last sit down to their meal. Their dinner is not so grand but Cook has made sure that there is plenty for all and that this poorer joint of beef which has had to roast slower and for longer has still some seasoning from her secret recipe. To Kate, the food lingers in her mouth, her taste buds luxuriating in flavours and smells that have never passed her lips before.

There is an enormous mountain of plates and utensils but as one the servants join together to wash up and stack it away, all the time singing songs and before Kate knows it the kitchen is clean as a whistle. Then Cook says to Kate that she can take the rest of the afternoon off but be back at seven.

Kate does not know what to do because she has never had any time of her own before. So she asks Cook, who replies, 'Why don't you take a wander around Thetford town and look at the shops?'

Kate changes back into her blue dress and walks into the town, now that she knows the way. After strolling the length of the high street in the warm afternoon sunshine she forms an opinion of Thetford. It is a pretty town, with its churches, shops and houses but the shops are closed and if they were open, what would she do with some meat from Tolly's butchers or bread from the Castle bakery? She already has all that she needs. Then she sees Webster's tailoring and dressmaking shop and the thought occurs that here is a place where she could buy a new dress for Sunday best. If she ever has any money of course.

There are other people walking around the town, old people, couples. Kate watches some children playing on the field, some game she has never seen and thinks to herself that this is normal, this is what people do and given time she can be just like them.

June 23rd

Some weeks later on an overcast summer morning Cook takes Kate outside to forage in the kitchen garden. Here she explains that the gardeners grow the vegetables that are used in some of the meals and would she like to pick some? Kate looks around at the neat rows of plants, they all look the same to her and she wonders where all these vegetables are, then to her astonishment Cook bends down and pulls at some foliage and a carrot appears. Then Cook takes Kate's hand and helps her to pull the next carrot out from the sandy soil. In a short while they have a couple of dozen large orange carrots with specks of soil, carefully arranged in a large wicker basket.

Next they are bending over some bushy plants and Kate follows Cook's example as she plunges her hand into the warm earth. Kate then pulls out a small potato with a covering so loose, that just by holding it in her hand the skin slips away and reveals the crisp white flesh beneath. After they have collected a basket of new potatoes, Cook takes her to a plant that has long green pods. Cook twists one off and pops the pod between her fingers to reveal large green beans and offers one to Kate to taste. The skin breaks easily in her mouth exposing the buttery sweet inner flesh. Kate says she has never tasted anything so lovely before.

'Your proper name is Green isn't it?' says Cook.

'It is, yes.' Kate replies.

'Well, I'm going to give you a pet name, my love. I'm calling you Bean from now on, because you are sweet.'

Kate blushed and smiled because she had never had a pet name. She was not even sure what one was but as they made their way back to the kitchen and met up with the other servants, Cook would keep on telling everyone Kate's new pet name and they were smiling and laughing on account of it. Kate was happy too, a contented kind of happiness because she was aware that Cook gave her the pet name because she likes her and Kate had never known this feeling before.

Later Kate is working through the routines of the day, dusting and polishing when the butler interrupts her endeavours.

'You have been here a while now, Miss Green,' he says, 'and your work is most satisfactory. You are diligent and conscientious.'

Kate smiles shyly, she is glad to hear that they are pleased with her.

'Cook tells me that she feels you have made very acceptable progress with the tasks that she has set you,' he continues, 'and therefore she would like you to become her apprentice, the under cook. In the light of this your probationary period is complete, your duties as an in-between maid are over and tomorrow you will start full time in the kitchen. Here is an envelope which contains your first proper pay packet and I am giving you permission to take the rest of the day off. Enjoy your afternoon, Miss Green.'

Kate's head is spinning from this news but it does not stop her from rushing to her room, changing into her blue dress and then running all the way in to the town. In Wells Street she finds Webster's the dressmakers and for a moment she has cold feet about entering such an imposing shop but Kate wants a dress, a dress that she has chosen, a dress that no one else has ever worn before and these thoughts impel her through the front door.

Inside, the main light comes from the windows behind her and the shop disappears into shadow. On each side are mahogany and glass cabinets with displays of hats and gloves and the shelves on the walls behind are filled with swatches of cloth. In the centre of the shop is a mannequin wearing a fine dress of shimmering sun coloured silk with tiny embroidered flowers. It towers over Kate but the effect is entrancing.

She states her requirements to an assistant. A fine dress for Sunday best is what she wants most of all, something that she could afford. She has nearly a pound on her and this was not going to be enough. However, any dress would take several weeks to make and there would be a fitting as well, so she could make payments in stages. Then there would be shoes and a hat and as the seasons change, a coat. Kate looked at the swatches of cloth and perused the dress designs before choosing a romantic design with a pretty cotton print of summer flowers which resembled the dress on the mannequin but was more to her pocket.

4th August

Kate is woken early because there is to be no bread delivery due to the bank holiday. Kate was told that she had been woken early on her first day many months ago so that Cook could assess her temperament. Temperament was a word that Kate had not encountered before but she was happy that they had thought it acceptable.

Together they mix the dough and then start kneading while singing a harvest hymn to keep the rhythm. Kate's voice is now strong and cheerful because she loves to work with Cook, especially when it is just the two of them. After they have sung 'We plough the fields and scatter' several times, Cook stops the kneading and then says, 'Bean, we're out of kindling for the bread oven, you need to go and find some so we can get it all going. Keep walking beyond the kitchen garden, there's plenty just lying around by the copse.'

Kate takes an old basket and a shawl. Outside the top branches of the trees glow in the golden light. The early morning air has a raw edge which causes Kate to wrap the shawl firmly around her shoulders. Beyond the copse Kate can see across the next field and in a hollow near the centre there are five haystacks of odd sizes that have been recently harvested. The haystacks are surrounded by a sea of mist and Kate takes a moment to fully contemplate the magical scene.

Then to Kate's left she sees a flock of sheep meandering down the slope with a young shepherd lad who is gently pushing them along. The day has barely begun and this shepherd looks chilled as though he has been out all night. In the still cold air she catches a tune and it makes her smile. He is singing an old folk song and his sweet young voice is full of both charm and mischief.

Kate settles down to gather twigs and small branches that will burn quickly and places them in her wicker basket. She is not sure how long she was collecting the kindling but when she looks up again she can see the shepherd lad has stopped near the haystacks and he is huddled over a small stack of hay and twigs himself, attempting to make a fire.

Kate returns to the house and gives the kindling to Cook to start the fire in the oven. The twigs are very damp because of the early morning dew and the kitchen soon fills with a smoky aroma. Cook brings the dough back to the marble worktop for a second knead when the footman enters the kitchen. He poses hands on hips, looking grand and handsome as he believes himself to be and says. 'Don't you know there has been a fire in the next field?'

'No,' says Cook. 'We haven't heard of no fire.'

Cook and Kate exchange glances but have to carry on kneading because otherwise the bread would not be ready in time for breakfast, so it takes a few more minutes before they can tin up the loaves and shape the bread rolls for the final rise. Cook then says to Kate. 'You go out for a look-see but just for a minute as there's still plenty to do.'

Kate rushes out of the kitchen and through the kitchen garden. In the next field the sheep are scattered to the four corners and being chased around by some young men. Down the in the hollow where the haystacks stood there is just blackened ground with smoke still rising. Beside the embers she can see a policeman, an old man and that young shepherd boy.

At the edge of the kitchen garden the two gardeners are deep in conversation. The older one says, 'I spoke to Jacob and he said that there'd been a barnburner sighted and this young lad had caught him in the act as it were and raised the alarm.'

The other says, 'I heard rumour of a barnburner Stowmarket way and it was a proper wicked thing to do but there's a lot of it about especially this harvest time.'

Then they see Kate and the older one asks. 'I hear you were outside earlier. Did you see anything?'

At first Kate is unable to find the words because she does not want to be the centre of attention, or, which would be even worse in her opinion, the cause of any trouble. Eventually she replies, 'I was busy picking up twigs.'

Later in the kitchen the haystacks fire is the only topic of conversation but Kate keeps what she saw to herself. The footman has been into the town and has heard some news which he is keen to relay. 'Old Tolly in the butcher's said that he heard that the police do not believe that the lad's story "attested to the facts on the ground" so they took him to the lock-up.'

Kate keeps quiet, it was none of her business and anyway, she reflected, she did not see the haystacks catch light and for all she knew a barnburner could have been the cause of the fire but that would be a remarkable coincidence.

Barnburner

Thetford, August 4, 1890

I told them a good story standing in that field but they don't believe me do they? A barnburner is a great story, especially when you've got no time to think.

There's the trouble though, no time to think. They have all the time in the world to do their thinking and ask questions that I can't answer. Where did he come from? Where did he go? How did he look? Was he carrying anything? Where were you? Where was he? What was he doing? Did he walk? Did he see you? Was he young? Was he old? I answered them as good as I could.

But I just confused them because they're not hearing the right answers. Then there's that constable, walking around, snooping. What's he doing looking at the burns in the ground? You can't trust a constable, because their heads are full of suspicion. Questions, questions. You said he lit the stack. I thought you said he was here? I thought he had a leather bag? This burn mark, there was a little fire here, how's that come about Master Bensley?

Was it you? The Inspector, he looks straight through me when he's speaking. The lies don't work on him, he just keeps on asking his questions. I can't hold back any more, I can't hide behind the lies, I can't do it. I'll have to tell them what happened.

It feels good to tell them, even though Pa will beat me and I'll lose my job and we need the money. They say I could go to gaol for arson. I'm only fourteen, don't want to go to no prison.

'Stand here,' they say. 'Stand straight, look at the bench.'

His Lordship is pompous isn't he just. I stand up and admit that I did it and then he says it's not good enough to tell a police inspector what I did. A judge needs to hear it properly.

Then the judge says, 'The crime is not whether Harry Bensley set the stack alight.'

Why does he say that? That is the crime, I did set the stack alight. I can't say I didn't set the fire because I'd be lying again.

He says, 'The crime is whether he did it wilfully and maliciously.'

I don't know what that means but it doesn't sound good. Wilful. They used to call me wilful in the schoolhouse so I could be that but I don't know. What are they thinking, the jury? Someone should tell them it's rude to stare. I can't look back at them. I get the fidgets in my feet and stare down at them.

Mr Hubbard, he's speaking up now. He's saying I'm a hard worker and at least I ran straight ways and told them there was a fire. That's good. That's a good thing to happen. Take a sideways look, the jury is listening.

His Lordship is summing up. It's not arithmetic which is how he makes it sound. He says I lit a fire to warm myself. That's right, that's what happened. Then he says that the haystacks burned in consequence. That's true too but is it a crime? Are you sending me to gaol?

The jury is deciding somewhere else and I have to wait. Sit on a plank and fidget because there is nothing else for me.

All rise, all rise, all rise. How do you find me? They are funny words, aren't they? Find me, look over here I'm standing in the dock, aren't I? Come on, tell me, I don't want to stand here all day.

'Not Guilty.'

That's me grinning, that's me, I'm not going to gaol. What's he saying, that judge? He's speaking now. A warning not to be so careless in future.

There's a truth. I won't be careless with fire and I won't be so careless with my stories either.

Waving

Thetford, 1891

As Kate collects vegetables in the early morning light she thinks about the questions that the other servants ask her about her family and her upbringing. Kate finds it easier to tell them that she is an orphan, even though it is not true, as her mother is very much alive and a well-known pest on the streets of Ipswich. Should Kate venture along those alleys she would recognise her mother but it is unlikely that her mother's milky eyes would recall her daughter. Rather she would beg her for pennies or lash out should she come too close without a brass farthing to offer.

Kate's father died many years earlier and that was the genesis of her mother's misery. While her mother's loss could only be anaesthetised by drink, the children were cast to the wind. At first the family of aunts and grandmas accepted the burden but soon the extra cost of the mouths to be fed and the realisation that this was no short term problem led to harsher treatment.

Despite this Kate finished school and then a miracle occurred. Her mother reappeared, clean and sober and what is more she has a vision for the family. She wants to bring them back together because she now has a house at a fair rent and work at a laundry and all due to a good citizen who is a leading light of the Baptist Church where she has foresworn her previous life and found redemption.

Kate's family is complete once more but something was lost in the original diaspora and that was the vital spark of happiness and contentment. The children have grown-up with lives and opinions of their own and soon the air is filled with the sound of quarrelsome adults and the most vocal and contrary of all was their mother.

Her mother's new work was hard and demanding with long hours and no respite but neither was home a place of peace. The only welcome was from her old friend the bottle. The consequences of which quickly followed, the rent went into arrears, the pantry emptied of food and the family were all evicted. Her brothers and sisters had work and found places they could stay but for Kate it became a choice between the poor house or the streets.

The poor house was not a terminus, not for a young girl such as Kate with her life in front of her, in fact she was free to leave at any time but to leave without a future would be foolish indeed. The long days of the workhouse regime were tough and unforgiving and the staff could be unkind, especially to strong willed adolescents. Kate quickly learnt to avoid the gaze of certain porters whose short temper would quickly lead to the use of their fat canes.

People would often arrive at the front gate looking for domestic servants and the most spiteful porter would escort them around. He had a face of blotches and scars that spoke of his inhumanity as he considered the inmates' only reason for existence was to benefit from a good beating. Kate would avoid his presence as much as possible but this day something strange and unusual happened.

Kate had seen the gentleman arrive at the gate and watched carefully as he is being taken around by the porter but there is something about this particular visitor that appealed to Kate. In her eyes he seems decent and fair and she can tell that he is not enjoying the company of his loathsome guide. As he walks around the workhouse his clothes are immaculate, without creases or stains, and he holds a tightly furled black umbrella with which he lightly taps the flagstones as he strolls along.

The tapping makes Kate look down and she is taken by an urge to find a clean cloth, then kneels down in front of the gentleman and polishes his shoes. Kate looks up and he is wide-eyed with astonishment, so she shows him the cloth and there on it is a smear of fresh mud but his shoes are now as bright and shiny as the rest of him. The look of astonishment slowly changes into a smile, a big friendly smile. He thanks the porter and the next thing Kate knows is she is leaving immediately to start work at a big house and that is how it all began.

That was over a year ago now and here is Kate lost in thought, so much so that she is surprised by a call of welcome from the next field.

'Good morn, to you.'

Kate looks up and sees a handsome young lad, unlike the servants at the hall who apart from the sullen hall boy are all of a different generation to her. He looks friendly and Kate thinks she does not mind if she makes his acquaintance.

'I know who you are,' she says. 'You're Haystacks Harry.'

There is a flash of weariness across Harry's face at the mention of the name that he is known by around the town and Kate sensing his reaction immediately regrets her flippant remark.

'Not you too,' he says in a quiet melancholic voice. 'I wish I could live that day different.'

Kate could see his pain and gently replied. 'I saw you, it was proper raw that morning. I saw you warm yourself.'

'And you never said nothing?'

'No one ever asked me.'

'I meant no harm.'

'I saw that too, Harry.'

'You have a kind heart but I still don't know your name.'

'I'm Kate.'

'Glad to make your acquaintance Kate. I hope we can be friends.'

Harry took down a sack that he was carrying over his shoulder and put a strong hand inside. He rooted around a bit and then with a flourish pulled out a ripe apple. He gave it a good old polish on a cloth and then offered it to Kate.

'Why thank you, I shall save it for later.'

Harry leant forward onto the fence between them and looked up at the big house. The kitchen garden wall cut off the view to the kitchen door but he could see the floors above.

'What do you do up at the Hall?' he says.

'I'm an under cook. So I am learning all about preparing food but when I'm not doing that I have to fill in with what jobs need doing, dusting, cleaning and polishing mainly. The house is amazing because they've just had electricity put in. I'm even allowed to turn on some of the lights, it's so exciting, no more scrabbling with a taper and the gas mantle. You just flick a switch as they say and there it is lit, bright as day.'

Harry's face took on a crooked look. 'I've seen the Hall all lit up at night from the field. It looks unnatural to me.'

'It's not unnatural, it's the future. They say everyone will have it in the future. I've even got an electric light in my room.'

'You have your own room?' He was amazed.

'That's the best thing, there's not much in it mind. Just a bed and a wardrobe for my clothes but it is my private little place. Although they do look in and make sure that I am keeping it spick and span. Look Harry, if you look up to the top floor, the second window along, that's my room.'

At that moment Kate felt something she had never experienced before because another person was jealous of her, her meagre possessions amounted to more than his.

'I wish I had a room of my own.' He says in a whisper. 'My family lives in one room and I've never even had a corner to call my own but I will, one day Kate I'll have a place and it will have electric and rooms, rooms for everyone and people will know me and I'll be famous and no one will call me Haystacks no more.'

Kate was not entirely sure what to make of this proclamation but before she could consider it too deeply she heard Cook calling from the kitchen door. So she tells Harry she has to hurry back and then the next thing he says is lovely and makes Kate feel warm inside.

'I'll wave to you, in your room, look out for me and I'll wave to you.'

Kate has to run back to the house but she turns back and can see Harry at the fence and he is waving furiously. She can't hide her smile but she dares not wave back because Cook has her eye on her now and she's waiting by the back door.

Harry was as good as his word though. That evening as dusk was closing in, Kate made her way to her room and before turning on the light she looked out of the window. There was Harry by the fence on the edge of Hubbard's field looking up and then he spots Kate at the window and he makes a huge smile and lovely friendly wave and Kate waves back, just a small wave. Then he turns and moves up the slope with his sheep.

From that day on Kate would look out for Harry. He wasn't always in the field but it made Kate's day when he was. It made her feel comfortable inside that someone was looking out for her, because until the day that she met Harry she never believed that anyone cared at all what happened to her.

There were times when Kate could find herself in the kitchen garden and see Harry and his flock in the field. If she was careful she could sneak down and catch a short conversation. Often on a Sunday Kate sees Harry as she goes to church and soon enough they are meeting up later in the afternoon to walk around the town. He's lovely and attentive to Kate and she feels so comfortable with him. As the months go by he begins to say that he loves her and as far as he is concerned she captured his heart that first cold morning he came over the hill with his sheep and set the haystacks ablaze but Kate thought that was just fanciful nonsense, because they are only young after all and Harry is the first boy she has met.

Cook and many of the servants up at the Hall have taken a shine to Kate because she is cheerful and hardworking but they have long known Harry's family and in particular they know about his father, who is well acquainted with the taverns of the town. They also think that Harry is a chip off the old block, a little rapscallion but Kate takes no notice of them because she is sure of Harry.

Dance

Thetford, July 1896

Just look at all the showman steam traction engines all rattling and humming to power those lights in the night sky. Many of them are Burrell's steam traction engines and they've all come back to Thetford where they were made, so it's a traction engine homecoming. I do hope they have a helter-skelter because they are proper fun. I do love a galloper, so please let there be a galloper for Kate and I to race in circles, holding hands.

They are setting up in the meadow by the river. It took them two days to roll up and now there's a lot of hustle and bustle as the colourful attractions are all put together. The fairground people look strong and sinewy and they speak funny too. I can watch it happening from out here on the slope and I know that everyone in the town is just bursting for the day when it opens.

Though I love Kate dearly I heard her say that she wants a dance when we go to the fair. I've not even got two left feet and I never know which way to go or where to put my hands when they call the dances. Amos Mosby said I should try a drink, that'll get my feet moving but I think that will just make my legs tangle up together and I'll end up looking foolish.

I can see the gallopers now. They have it all lit up in the meadow and they are looking to see if it all works properly. Should we do it first or last? Both, I've got enough money because I've been saving ever since the notices went up all over the town and I'm going to need a pretty purse to keep my Kate entertained. Kate says she don't mind if it's a Dutch treat but I do. I want to look after her good and proper. I'll be so proud walking with her, going from stall to stall, letting her do what she wants.

Up goes the helter-skelter. You'd never know it could be there when they come in their bright wagons. How can they hide a huge tower in them? It's like watching a magician at work. I so want it to be tomorrow and then I want tomorrow to last forever.

Kate says all the staff at the Hall have got the afternoon off to go to the fair and I am not shepherding until the night. I wait by the field gate to the fair, turning up early at one o'clock because I long to spend every moment with my Kate. I can see the gallopers turning to the music and hear the noise of the steam engines and laughter and chatter of the crowd but I can't see my Kate.

She turns up at quarter past three all out of breath and full of apologies but wearing a pretty blue dress that she had just bought from the dressmakers. She says that it took longer than she thought to pick it up, especially as she was not the only one who had a new dress to collect that day. Never mind, I say we have the rest of the afternoon and we take off around the stalls. My purse is full of money and I'm paying a penny here and a penny there, it seems a small amount but they soon add up to something. We have a try at the gallopers which set my head in a spin and we were both rolling about and giggling after.

I drag Kate over to the helter-skelter but when we get close and she sees it all, she says she's afraid of heights. I want to have a go but I won't do it without her, so we walk on by and then Kate says she would like a dance. I don't want to say that I fear dancing as much as she fears the helter-skelter. I muster my courage as we make for the dance floor.

I can hear the fiddle music before we see the dancers, there's an accordion player and a caller as well. Kate's very excited and drags me onto the floor before I even got to see what the dancing looks like. Kate always says that when she hears music her feet just can't stop moving.

The fiddler and accordion player take up a tune and there's lots of couples all in a line and we join the end of it, then the caller sings out the steps. I am standing there trying to look as though I'm in the right place but inside I'm feeling lost.

'Couples to the corners, here we go, take your partner, one, two, three and gallop to the opposite, one, two, three and turn around one, two, three and back to where you started, one, two, three.'

Kate's full of joy, more than I've ever seen before, so I try to copy the others and we just avoid a nasty crash on the way back and then the caller cries out in his sing-song voice. 'Into the centre one, two, three and right hand star.'

Everyone else seems to know what to do, anyway I put my hand up into the centre and then I turn and walk the wrong way and everyone is looking and sniggering. I carry on though because Kate is full of smiles.

'Now, turn around and left hand star.'

They all turn around and I'm looking the wrong way again, I can feel my blood coming up but I am going to try though I am feeling such a misfit.

'Now do-si-do your partner's partner.'

I'm all clumsy and we knock heads, so that's it, I can't do it, I just can't do it. It feels as though they have made this all up to laugh at me and I need to get away. I take off and find the cider stall where I can hide away but then I realise I've left Kate behind.

I have to find her so I walk around the fair looking for her brown hair and pretty new blue dress but I can't see her at any of the stalls, then I do the one thing I don't want to do and go back to the dance floor and I spy Kate there but I don't have to spy because I can see her, bold as, and she's dancing with another man.

I am not staying when I am not wanted.

Scuffle

Thetford, May 1897

When Cook makes pastry it looks so easy. She measures out some cups of flour, chops in some lard and dabbles water into the mixing bowl and then gently kneads it with her firm hands to make the smoothest, lightest pastry. Kate is trying to do the same, she's never made pastry by herself but Cook has left her to make the dough for a steak and kidney pie.

Kate looks at her pastry mix, instead of being smooth it is a pile of crumbs, so Kate splashes some drops of water into the bowl and carries on kneading. The mixture is coming together but now it becomes sticky and stretches and Kate is even less confident of her work.

Cook bustles in from the town and she is bursting with news.

'Bean, my Bean.' She says. 'Your Harry was seen coming out of the train station around ten this morning'.

Kate was lost for words, she felt strangely disorientated.

'When I was buying the meat in the butchers, Mr Tolly told me that the stationmaster saw Harry come off the Cambridge train and his ticket had been bought in London. What do you make of that Bean?'

Kate's mind was a jumble of thoughts, ever since the fair she had waited for news of Harry but no one had seen him since that day. It was as if the fair had magicked him away and even his father would declaim in the public house that Harry had left them all in the lurch as they needed his money to pay the rent. Kate was sure that Harry's disappearance was her fault, although many people said that his father's tavern talk was mainly to get others to loosen their purse.

Dancing had always been a good friend to Kate, giving her one of her most treasured memories. A summer's day, a field of hay, the long day's work complete and hearing music in the distance. All the workers and their children were drawn towards the melody, there was joy and laughter, it seemed that time itself was stopped as Kate felt the music flow through her and her whole body fill with delight.

At the fair those thoughts were rekindled as the music had drawn Kate to the dance floor. Although she had sensed some reticence from Harry, she was sure that once his feet started to move he was bound to feel the same way. As the dance progressed she could see that he was struggling to find his rhythm, or to find any rhythm. Not that Kate was unhappy, sometimes the music can be elusive. Kate is dancing with her partner's partner and when she turns to rejoin Harry, he's just not there. For a moment Kate believes that Harry has made another wrong turn as he has not managed one correct move in the whole dance so far but then she looks around and she is alone on the dance floor.

Cook can see that Kate is lost in her own thoughts and helps her to sit down, then she sees the dough and laughs.

'What have you done here with this pastry, Bean? You've been working it too hard, my little love and that'll never do. I'd better start over because I don't think we can rescue that but you take notice while you're sitting there.'

'I can't just stay here, though.'

'Oh, I think you should, you shouldn't be rash. Now that you know he's here you should think on what words you want to say to him, if anything at all, or more to the point what you need to hear from him. I think he owes you an honest story and you trying to find him lets him off the hook, so to speak. You just sit and watch me make pastry and give that some thought, my love.'

Kate watches the mixing and kneading but her mind is elsewhere and all she wants to do is get answers to her questions. To know why he left her, where he's been all this time, why he's come back and in her heart she feels that if she hears the right answers it can all be mended. Although she does not know how the right answer should sound, because she cannot think of a good reason for him leaving that way.

Except she can. The green-eyed monster got him because after standing alone waiting for Harry to return another young lad had asked her to dance. While they were dancing she glanced up and saw Harry in the crowd and the look on his face as he spotted here on the dance floor. There is no doubt it is all her fault, making him dance in front of all those people when he never wanted to and Kate knew it inside her. So Kate stands up and says to Cook.

'I'm sorry but I have to go and find him.'

Kate puts on her raincoat and sets off to the town. Cook is very concerned but says she will let the butler know Kate needed some time off. It wouldn't be a problem, she said because Kate never had any particular time for herself since Harry left.

Now Kate is walking past the Wells Street shops and turning into Kings Street beside the Church. She can see people looking her way and pointing at her and she is unused to being the centre of attention. She walks up and down Magdalene Street but Harry's not about. Then she realises that she should go to his father's house because that is probably where he would visit first.

Kate turns the corner into St Giles' Lane where can see a commotion of men in the distance and Henry Webster from the tailoring shop is hollering at a police constable. The constable is kneeling on the back of a man who is pinned down on the ground and there is struggling and scuffling between them. Then the prostrate man raises his eyes and looks up at Kate, catches her face and stops his struggle.

Mimic

Thetford, July 1897

They say I'm a fool to have gone back but how was I to know they'd remember? It was ages ago. You'd think the tailor would have long forgotten about it and then when the manager from the Co-op chipped in and said I stole some clothes as well, that just made it worse. How did they think I was going to go off to London without new clothes? All right, I admit I didn't pay for them but I was going to make amends if they had a given me a moment. Then when I say I'd just come out from choky in the Big Smoke and I'd done my time, that just made it worse. So here I am, having to stand up in Thetford courtroom with all the town looking on and Kate of course. She was there looking so pretty, that was wrong, dammit. She shouldn't see my disgrace.

I admitted it. I admitted it straight away, because I don't want a fuss and thought it'd all be dealt with but it wasn't dealt fair and it wasn't dealt right. Then they tell the whole courtroom that I'd been in prison for six months for theft. I can see Kate with her long brown hair and lovely eyes but she's calculating in her head and she's working out that six months is most of the time I was away. That's the last I saw of her though, they took me back down to the cell and then off to Norwich once the sentencing was over.

They put you in solitary when you first arrive. If I stretch my arms out I can touch both sides of my cell. I have a window that has no view even if I stand on my bed, just a brick wall. I can hear though, lots of banging doors and shouting, there's plenty of shouting. At night I am glad of the darkness because it goes quiet at last. After a month they took me out and put me in another cell. I'm still on my own, but now the hard labour starts. I didn't have that in the Scrubs. You are not allowed to speak or it's back to solitary, just have to work, tedious back-breaking work on a big wheel. Ten minutes on, five minutes off, walking, walking, walking until you can't walk any more but you have to keep walking or they take you off to the whipping-frame and beat you before bringing you back to the treadmill to trudge on. Saw a man drop right in front of me as I was taking a rest. He was walking the treadmill, then collapsed clutching his heart and fell into the wall to be battered by the steps. The warders dragged him out and lay him down but he was gone, quick as.

One night I get back to the cell and I'm not alone any more. I can't make this new fellow out, he's all dainty and neat. Not at all like the other prisoners. He keeps himself clean and he has no edge. I don't rate his chances.

He's a strange one and no mistake. We all call him Lord Claude on account of him speaking as if he has a plum in his mouth. I've heard such talk but I've never had to listen to it all night. He talks about his comings and goings all the time as if it were important. He sneered at me at first as a son of the soil but I soon put him right. In here we are all the same I say, it's us versus them. You start trying to pull class and it will be you in deep trouble.

He's never been in prison before so he doesn't know the ropes but he soon learns that there is no privilege inside. There's no birthright to respect, you need to earn it and you earn it from the older lags who know all the tricks. You can rub along just fine if you've got something to trade. I don't have much to trade but then I don't get much attention. Lord Claude meanwhile, he's in everyone's eye, because of his way of speaking. They all think he must have a fortune.

So I say to him, 'What are you in for and don't tell me no lies because we're all innocent in here, even me who pleaded guilty.'

So he says, 'Embezzlement.'

I say, 'I don't know what that means.'

He replies 'It's similar to stealing money.'

I say, 'Well I did that but it didn't have no pretty name.' Then he laughs.

I say, 'How do you know all these fancy things?'

He says, 'It's my education.'

I say, 'I had a schooling but I never learnt nothing highfalutin like that.' And he laughs again.

A day or two later and it is supper time and Lord Claude is taking his plate and spoon back when I notice he's been followed by a couple of the hard-tack prisoners. I've got a nose for trouble so I get up and walk a little way behind them. They grab Claude and force him to the ground, one of them has his arm in a lock while the other is holding a knife to his throat and he's whispering. I can't hear what he's saying but it is plain that it terrifies poor Claude. I don't want to be a tell-tale and I can't tackle them alone so I have to think quick. I see an empty bench nearby and I kick it hard so it clatters loud over to where Claude is being held and the gaolers look round to see what's what. They move as quick as quicksilver and they corner the hard-tack with the knife but he's not got rid of it and makes menacing lunges at the gaolers. In a flash one of the gaolers throws his coat over the knife hand and the rest bring him down. He's off to the whipping cage and then solitary but the other one got clean away.

'What's that about?' I say to Claude later in the cell.

'They heard I stole a lot of money and they want a cut so they'll protect me in here. Otherwise bad things will happen.'

That's true, if a bad sort has an eye on you, they can make life devilish hard.

I say, 'Do you have any money?'

He replies, 'Of course not, they took it all when they caught me.'

I say, 'You're not telling me no lies are you?'

He replies, 'I think I can trust you, they found every penny.'

So I say, 'I think I can trust you too and that's the best you can hope for in here. You stick by me and I'll keep my eye on you.'

Lord Claude looks properly grateful and then he says, 'I will attempt to reciprocate this arrangement.'

Now I laugh. Attempt to reciprocate the arrangement. That sounds proper posh and I repeat it out loud as if he had said it. Then I say, 'Just keep an eye out, just keep an eye out.'

We speak a lot in the evenings from then on and Lord Claude tells me about his life. He's lived in a big house and had servants and all that. His father went to India to be some bigwig. So Claude was sent away to a place called a boarding school where he stayed all year. Then he went to university, where there is even more learning. Finally his father found him work in a company in London and he had a fine life going to dances and drinking. He also joined a gentleman's club and this was his downfall because they love a gamble, those gentlemen and he could not stop himself. He was making wagers on cards, on horses, if two snails were racing he'd put down a bet. It turned out that he just loved the risk of a wager.

That's how he came to embezzling. If you lose a bet you have to pay up and when you don't have the necessary there are people, nasty people, who will put the bite on you. As luck would have it, at the same time he was sent up to Norwich on company business. When he got there he saw a ripe opportunity to syphon off, as he called it, some funds from this little business. His plan was that once he'd paid his debt and won some money back he was going to make it all square but he was caught out too soon. Then he admitted that the two ruffians who had approached him earlier had made mention of the name of the bookkeeper who held his debts in London and made it plain that he wanted them cleared, so he was a worried man.

'That's a predicament and no mistake.' I say and then I says, 'I never used a word like predicament before.'

Lord Claude laughs and says, 'I must be rubbing off on you.'

Then he makes a really strange comment. He says, 'You know you are a good mimic?'

I ask him what he means and he says, 'I think you would make a good actor, with your ear for being a copycat.'

He asks me to tell him about my life, so I tell him about home, which is a room with my pa and my brothers. I tell him about the miserable schoolhouse. Then I tell him about working as a shepherd and the haystacks that I didn't mean to burn down because I was just cold and I made a fire that got out of hand and before I know it I'm in big trouble. I say that's what happens to me, I'm hotheaded and don't think things through.

Then I tell him about Kate, how I met her and used to wave to her every day from the field, how we were sweethearts and I says I miss her so and I've made such a fool out of myself because of a stupid fair, because of a stupid dance, because of my stupid mind thinking terrible jealous thoughts that made me leave her and get in trouble. I just went crazy and ran off to London but I stole some clothing before I left from a shop because I didn't have no money for nice clothes. They say that London is paved in gold but I only saw pigeon droppings. I can't find work, my pockets are empty and I get hungry, then I see this man and he shows his purse on the street and I'm nearby and I got the urge to snatch it but I hadn't planned it, because if I had thought ahead I would've had a good look round first. There were peelers everywhere and I get chased but they can run much faster than me and there's more of them. That's when I get put inside the first time, six months in the Scrubs. Easier than this though because there was no hard labour. Then they let me out and I come back home thinking I've done my time and they arrest me straight off. That ruins all my plans because I want to make things straight with my sweetheart if she'll have me and I can't do that from in here.

That's when he says, you could write her a letter and I say, I could but my writing is none too proper, I always got told how bad it was. He says he'll help me, he says tell me what you want to say and he'll write it down properly and then I can copy it out in my own hand. There's a way and no mistake. Lord Claude says he's got some paper, pen and ink and he shows me a little leather case and there they are. I say, I'll have to think about what I want to say as I'm none too clever with words and he says just tell me and I'll see what words we could use.

I say, I want to tell her that I made a bad mistake and should never have gone away. I still love her and I miss her. I hope that she can love me again. So he starts to write and then he strikes out a few words here and there and then he gives me the letter to copy out.

My Darling Kate,

I know this will be a surprise for you but it is my fervent hope that you will read this letter and consider its contents carefully. I know you are a forgiving person and I also know that many people would regard my recent actions as unforgivable. However, my dearest Kate, you have a big heart, big enough to allow me this small opportunity to explain myself.

I wish I could dance because I would stay in your arms forever. I wish I was nimble and sleek of foot. I wish I was slow to rise to jealousy and unworthy thoughts and most of all I wish that I could undo everything I did in consequence. I am truly sorry for everything that happened.

I know I have fallen a long way but if you have any feelings for me, then send me a sign and I will do anything you ask to win your approval once more. If, however you no longer wish to see me, then regretfully I would say that I fully understand and will trouble you no further.

I am still the boy that waved to you.

Yours Truly

Harry

It was a beautiful letter though I was troubled by the part about not seeing me again but he says if there is no hope you need to know. I copy it out and send it off the next day and a few days later I got a letter in reply. Kate wrote and said how moved she was by my words and that she would wait for me until I was let out and we would talk about the future.

I tell all the people that I know that I got this reply and it was good and I tell them that Lord Claude wrote the words for me and they worked as if they were magic balm. That's a skill and no mistake. Soon all sorts are turning up and needing nice letters written and Lord

Claude is making a lovely little living with his trade, earning tobacco and other comforts. He also gains some respect and even the hard-tacks are leaving him alone because one of them needs a letter to his lawyer and Lord Claude said he would help him if there was no more unpleasantness while he was inside.

I came on strong with my mimicry. I could impersonate some of the warders which would make the others laugh but best of all I could carry off posh. Lord Claude and me would impersonate a couple of swells out on the town and that would have them rolling about.

I've made it sound as though prison was a barrel of laughs but it was far from. There was many a broken man from the hard labour. Claude made it possible for me to survive. Most importantly he helped me win back Kate and at the same time I learned all about the rich man's world. In many ways meeting Claude was the turning point of my life.

Fits

Stepney, February 1901

'You had better sit down, Mrs Bensley.'

The relieving officer is sitting behind a large wooden desk, at the front of which is a rack of official looking stamps and an ink pad. He is thin and spiky. He avoids Kate's gaze as scrapes the inside of the bowl of a pipe with a knife which once he has finished cleaning it out to his satisfaction, he then gently rests in an ashtray. His spindly arm moves to take a printed form from a pile on his right. He adjusts his eye glass on his long sombre face so he can better read the first question. He speaks as though he has never seen this form before.

'So tell me your full name'

'Katherine Bensley, sir.'

'And your age?'

'I'm twenty five.'

The relieving officer repeats the words as he writes them down on the form in his large copperplate script.

'And where were you born?'

'I was born in Ipswich, sir.'

'You were born in Ipswich? And yet I hear you're from Thetford.'

'Yes, sir I was taken to Thetford when I was fourteen.'

'Under what circumstances Mrs Bensley did you move to Thetford?'

'I was an orphan in Ipswich, sir. I moved to Thetford when I was employed by the Hall as a maid.'

'Were you in an orphanage?'

'I was, sir, in a way. My father died when I was very young and my mother had difficulties looking after us so she would often place us children in the poorhouse.'

'And in Thetford? Tell me more about what happened in Thetford.'

'Well, as I said, I worked at the Hall as a maid. After a while they made me the under cook.'

'So they valued you, you were a hard worker?'

'They were always satisfied with my work, sir, if that's what you're asking.'

'If, as you say, you were well employed in Thetford then answer me this. Why did you come to London?'

'I married, sir. I married Harry Bensley.'

'Harry Bensley? That was the man I just interviewed, you married him even though he is a convicted criminal?'

'I've known Harry since I was fourteen, he's been very foolish as a young man and done plenty of bad things but I do know that I love him and that he didn't mean to do those things. We married because he promised me that he had changed and would not do wrong again and since we have been married he has made every effort to be a good Christian man.'

'So I ask again Mrs Bensley, why have you come to London?'

'I know he has changed because he's good to me and to the children but the other people in Thetford they don't see it, they still think he's a bad seed who will bring me nothing but misery. They are unkind to him and to all of us. Harry can't find work, not any work that will last more than a few days. So we are always living from hand to mouth. In the end Harry says, 'We should go to the smoke and try our luck'. That's why we left Thetford, to come up to London and find better work, because as Harry says, 'People don't know me here' and that means we can have a second chance which they won't give us in Thetford.'

'I see. You have come to London for a second chance and do you know people here?'

'Yes, sir, Harry has some friends that he made before when he was in London and we hoped they might be able to help us. We just haven't been able to find work sir and there aren't many folk who can put up a whole family for a long period of time.'

'Yes, you said you had a family. You'd better tell me all of the details.'

'I've two little girls, sir. There's Alice, she's nearly two years old and there is little Lily, who is just a baby.'

'I suppose you'll be expecting us to take them in as well?'

'I won't be parted from them, sir. I will stay on the street rather than that.'

'Turning to other matters, your husband, Mr Bensley, he reported that he collapsed on the street. Can you tell me what happened as he seemingly has no memory of the particulars the event?'

'Yes, sir, we were told of a place where we might be able to find boarding near Stepney Green. We walked over here carrying all our possessions from Vauxhall and we found the house and enquired about the room but the landlord took against us sir and said he didn't take in young families and told us to be gone. We stood there, not knowing what to do and that's when Harry took his turn. He collapsed sir, he just felt the ground and his body was shaking and writhing. I was at a loss but as fortune would have it there was a constable nearby and he came and soothed Harry. After a few moments Harry came to and the constable asked us what had happened here. I told him that we had come looking for a place to stay but there was no space for us and it was the constable who had the idea to bring us here.'

At that moment there was a knock on the door. The relieving officer's solemn face looked up from the form for the first time.

'Come in.'

A thin streak of a girl in a starched uniform with a pristine white pinny came into the room. She stood with an expectant but fearful look on her face. Finally she spoke. 'I'm sorry to interrupt you sir but there has been an incident. The man who was just admitted has suffered a collapse in the bathing room and matron and the porter are taking him over to the infirmary.'

Kate clutched at her heart when she heard this. The sombre faced man started rifling through some of the papers in the pile to his left. He picked one up and examined it with great care, satisfied, he then grasped one of the wooden handled brass stamps on the rack in front of him and held it firmly on the ink pad. Then with a flourish and loud bang he stamped the paper. The word 'Infirmary' now indelibly marked on Harry Bensley's form. He then looked Kate squarely in the face.

'Has your husband had a history of fainting, Mrs Bensley?'

Kate stared at him and gasped and finally shook her head.

'I see.'

'I want to go to him.'

'Before we can admit you to the workhouse we must complete your form and then there are some necessary procedures to be followed. Let's see now. Your maiden name?'

Carman

Croydon, June 1901

They don't want it. It says it's for them on the delivery papers but they say they never ordered it. Here we go, lovely job, it's a bit of lost property. I just need to get a message to Morris to meet me under the round tower at the Leslie Arms. I'll send the boy to get him.

I wonder what I'll get. The papers here say it's a gilt wall mirror. I've had a peek inside and I can see an ornate frame and a bevelled mirror that would grace many a front room. Just the kind of lost property he's looking for, so now Morris just needs to lose the papers back at the office and we can claim it for our own.

I sent the boy off with the message, gave him a thruppeny piece and told him to stay shtum. He looks happy with it but I've only spent a couple of runs with this lad so it's better he doesn't know what this is about until I am sure of him. I lead the horses up to the water trough and let them get a good drink.

A carman, this is the best job. Lord Claude, bless him, he really pulled out all the stops to get us out of the workhouse when he got my letter and now I've got my ticket on the lost property racket I can make more money than I ever take in tips. Tips are good, now I've got my act down pat. Give them the old soft soap and they fall for it, especially the old ladies, they love a refined gentleman delivering their goods. You just have to find an in, as they say.

Oh, I would rather not put this sideboard down on that splendid rug. Is it Indian? I thought as much, I've not been to India but my father is there now, he's in charge of the Indian Office in Bangalore. I really don't know much about what he does but I'm sure it's very important. Is here good for you? I think you have an excellent eye for decor, madam. You were in India for twenty years? How lovely for you but you're glad to be back. We are very happy to see you today. Thank you, that is most generous. Good day madam, we look forward to your business in the future.

Servants are the worst though. They won't pay a tip of course, maybe a butler will if you are lucky or you will get a cup of tea and a bit of bread in the kitchen but they see straight through the accent. Some of them whisper things. 'I know your game, farmer's boy.' While others look at you like the warders at the workhouse. I don't think it's good enough yet to fool them. Or maybe they just don't believe the idea of a carman having class. Whatever it is, it doesn't work but there is no profit in fooling them anyway.

Kate has always wanted a fine mirror. It's a shame we can't keep it but Morris says you can't keep lost property. Lost property needs to turn up somewhere else, not in the carman's house that was delivering it. If lost property is found there then the police will start asking difficult questions, because the police don't have the right idea about lost property, they think it still belongs to someone. I've already had dealings with the police so that discussion would go only one way.

We have the right idea though. Once something is missing, that's it, it can't be found because it's lost. In our way we are providing a service. Otherwise it would only go back to the storehouse and then back to the maker, which is just letters and storage and packing and repacking. Far better for lost property to stay lost and cause no further mischief.

There has been a lot more lost property recently. I've seen Morris drinking with a gentleman from bought ledger in the Leslie Arms I'm not sure what that means but whereas it used to be one or two items a month, now it can be once or twice a week. Morris was saying he might be able to tell me what will be lost property before it even arrives, which would be clairvoyant. At the same time, although there is more lost property, my cut keeps reducing. Seems to me that the cut should be bigger because the risk happens more frequently. It's going to need words with Morris.

The boy's back. Gives me a note. It's not good. Morris can't meet me. He says, can I take it somewhere safe and he will arrange to have it picked up tonight? I could take it back home, that's the only option. I give the boy a note for Morris and head for home.

I've got to have a good reason, something she'll see the truth in. It's no big deal, I'll say, just a little hiccup in the day. I need some more space in the back as I've just had word they need a large item moved urgently and I thought it would be easy to drop this off here and get it picked up later.

That look on her face, she is more than a bit perturbed. You've not done this before, she says. There's always a first time for everything, Kate. It will all be tidied up by tonight, don't worry yourself, I'm taking care for all of us.

Kate has told me never to lie but I'm not lying I'm just not telling her the whole picture, which is not the same thing at all. I have to protect her and if the best way to do that is to leave out some details then that is what I will do. I promised you Kate I would not lie to you and I am keeping my word.

Morris isn't coming tonight, he is sending some fellows to pick it up. It's worth my while as it keeps me in the lost property racket. I've not seen this fellow nor his mate before and they look shifty. Kate's not liking this one bit but she's keeping her tongue. Glad to see them go though.

It's nothing Kate, it's nothing to worry about. Sometimes we have to do things in a hurry and this was the best way. It will all turn out for the good. I would tell you if there is a problem but there is no problem. I've not met those fellows before, they must be on the evening staff but they knew what they were doing and there is no problem now. I promised, yes I promised I wouldn't lie to you and believe me I'm not lying now. I can't answer that because I don't know the right answer. In business things don't work that way, Kate. Sometimes you have to do something extra and this was just one of those occasions. It won't happen again. No, don't say that, I'm telling you what it is best for you to hear. No, I didn't mean it that way, I am not hiding something, I don't know the answer to that question either. I'm not lying to you. I'm not lying to you. I would not lie to you.

I'm gone.

Policeman

Thetford, August 1904

A bowler-hatted stranger with a battered brown leather case is standing at the door and he asks for Kate by name. She does not often get visitors, working as she does as a housekeeper and nanny for the local doctor, let alone strangers asking for her. Kate looks over the outsider, he's an uncommon looking man with blotchy red rugged skin and a formal gentleman's handlebar moustache that struck her as out of place on that craggy face.

'I'm looking for a Mrs. Kate Bensley. I understand she works here?'

Kate replies, 'I was Mrs. Kate Bensley, though I have now taken back my original name and I now ask people to call me Miss Kate Green.'

He looks a bit taken aback by this and then he says, 'Well, er, let me introduce myself, I'm Detective Sergeant Cole from Paddington Police Station in London. I need to ask you some questions about your ... your ex-husband.'

This completely confuses Kate and she stands at the door clasping and unclasping the handle, then she realises that she had better ask her employer if she can invite the detective sergeant into the house. Leaving the policeman at the door she goes into the front room and asks Mrs Minns if it would be acceptable for him to come in. Mrs Minns replies, 'You had better take him to the kitchen and I will make sure the children are kept occupied.'

Kate leads the detective through the house into the back kitchen where she prepares the meals. There are vegetables laid out ready to be prepared for dinner, which Kate moves aside before they sit down around the main table. He says he wants to make some notes and takes out a notebook and an ink pen. Kate is unable to hide her

curiosity any longer and asks, 'Why have you come up all this way to
see me?'

'I've got some questions for you about your husband.'

'I've not set eyes on him for nigh on two years, sergeant, I don't
think I know anything that can help you.'

'Let's start from the beginning. Your name is...'

'Kate Green.'

'So have you been married, Miss Green?'

'Well, I was, yes. I was married to Harry Bensley.'

'And when did you marry him?'

'I married him nearly five years ago on the 6th August 1898.'

'And do you have a marriage certificate?'

'We certainly had one, sergeant. I expect it will be in one of my
boxes upstairs from when I moved back up to Thetford. There are
things I've not looked at since we got back from London.'

'Can you find it please? I would like to see it.'

Kate went upstairs and the sergeant followed, which she did not
think was the gentlemanly thing to do, to enter a lady's bedroom.
When Kate had left London she had placed what was left of her
possessions in tea chests and she had a pretty table cloth covering
them up. She removed it and opened up the top of one of the chests
and inside there were some papers, in amongst them was the
marriage certificate which she gave to the inspector. He read the
details thoroughly.

'I see, the date is right here and these people, Edgar Elma and Lily
Elma, your witnesses, they still live locally?'

'Lily has married, she married Amos Mosby and she lives in London
now but we still write to each other.'

'Her address would be helpful.'

'I've just got a letter from her recently, here it is. Look, there's her
address on the top here.'

'So according to this certificate you married in August 1898. When
did you last see your husband?'

'I last saw him in June two years back, he left me...'

'...he left you. So have you, have you divorced your husband?'

'I wouldn't know where to start such an enterprise. Anyway I don't know where he is, I've not seen nor heard from him since.'

'So the facts are that you are still married to Harry Bensley?'

'On paper, I suppose I am.'

He wrote something down in his notebook, then flicked back a couple of pages and read something to himself, then glanced up and asked Kate 'Tell me, what do you know of a Mr. Henry Burrell?'

'Henry? Henry Burrell? I can't say that I have heard of him. There is the Burrell family, everyone knows of them, they run the steam traction engine factory in the town but I don't know their names.'

'No ... Henry ... Burrell. Right. Well, look, there is going to be a trial and we might have to call you as a witness.'

'A witness? A witness to what, sergeant? I don't know what all these questions are all about. What am I supposed to have done?'

At this the sergeant looked very confused and surprised.

'You've not read the papers then. I would have thought it would have been the talk of the town.'

'I don't have time for newspapers, I'm no lady of leisure, anyway there is never a mention of anything of interest to someone like me.'

The sergeant leans down and brings up his leather case, the clips spring open and he reaches in and brings out a copy of The Times of London. He opens it and folds it into a third and then points to an article. Handing it over to Kate he says, 'I think this will be of interest to you.'

Heir

Excerpt from: The Cole Report

The notable cases of Chief Inspector George H. Cole of the Metropolitan Police.

Part 7: The heir, apparently

The story begins in June of 1902, as Henry Burrell, a man in his late twenties, medium height and well-built walks into the Duke of Clarence public house in South Norwood. His first act on entering is to buy a drink for the regulars at the bar and he soon engages them in conversation, telling them that though he is a gentleman, his father had sent him off from the family home to get a proper working education. Now he is employed as a carman for a department store whose owner he claimed was known to his father. He tells them how much he is enjoying his new surroundings and how much more trustworthy and hardworking the people he meets today are than those toffs he met at school. Who, he opines, know nothing of real life and are unworthy recipients of the silver spoon. This tale goes over well with the people at the bar but it is not them he wants to impress. Taking the orders for the drinks and lingering to listen to the conversation of this stranger is a very attractive young woman, Lily Clapham who had recently begun working as a serving girl in the public house.

After about an hour of conversation and drinking with his new friends, Burrell breaks away from the group and asks Miss Clapham if she had a free evening soon and invites her out for dinner and a dance. Lily replies properly that she makes it a rule never to go out with any man when she does not know their name. He introduces himself as Mr Henry Burrell, grandson of the famous steam traction engine factory owner Charles Burrell of Thetford.

Miss Clapham meanwhile has overheard something in the conversation between the group at the bar and is eager to hear more details about his life before agreeing to an evening out.

'What's all this I hear about you being the son and heir?'

'I will be,' says Burrell, 'but right now I'm just an ordinary fellow making my way in the world. Learning from the 'bottom up' as my father put it to me before I left the stately old pile for London. The advantage is that I get to enjoy the company of real people, not the Pall Mall Percys of my father's set and look around you, look at how much joy has come this evening. Then to cap it all, my eyes are given the delight of seeing you, surely the most perfect being walking this earth today. I am sure you must dance divinely and I feel duty bound to take you out.'

He certainly could talk and Miss Clapham was unable to resist his charms. Not that she had any inclination to do so, in comparison to the drab clientele of the Duke of Clarence public house, Burrell was a very exotic beast indeed.

He woos Miss Clapham, going out for dinner and a dance twice maybe three times a week, not something that a person on a carman's wages would be able to afford very often. We can only speculate that he was able to supplement his income through goods going missing from the back of his cart, petty larceny being a common occupational benefit of many a dishonest carman. When he was not dining and dancing, his profligate lifestyle continued at the Duke of Clarence public house, where he would 'stand a round' for his new found friends, all the time hinting at his extraordinary wealth just out of reach.

One of the men at the bar was a Mr Thomas Jordan. Burrell confided in Mr Jordan that he was unhappy with his present employment as he was outside in all weathers. Mr Jordan happened to be a locomotive inspector and he was in a position to offer him employment as a stoker. Back-breaking work but it seems that this son of the gentry was keen to take it on.

His friends at the bar were eager to hear more about his previous life and Burrell was more than happy to oblige. He told them he was the 'son and heir' but not to his father's fortune, although that was significant because everyone knew of Burrell steam traction engines. He told them that he was to inherit a large and lucrative farm owned by his Aunt who had recently passed away. The farm was variously reported to consist of a thousand to twelve thousand acres of productive farm land with a nine to twelve thousand pound a year income, sums beyond the dreams of the loungers at the bar.

At the same time his dalliance with Miss Clapham continued apace. She left her job at the Duke of Clarence and moved into rented rooms with Burrell despite the disapproval of her family. As sure as night follows day, nature takes its course and Miss Clapham becomes pregnant before marrying Burrell at Marylebone Registry Office.

Burrell is confiding more about his inheritance to his new employer, Mr Jordan. He claims that he is unable to access any money due to a clause in the will that only allows the estate to be entrusted to him on his thirtieth birthday, two years hence.

Miss Clapham by now gives birth to a baby boy and Burrell's real money worries are more troubling. He also starts to act erratically, coming home late at night, pacing about and not sleeping. He is evasive when she asks him simple questions, such as where he has been or what he has been doing.

Back at his employers meanwhile, Burrell is revealing yet more details about the complexities behind his inheritance. He tells his new boss that he has had a very sad correspondence from his sister. Her Doctor has told her that she is very sick with consumption and her health would be greatly restored by a sea cruise. He dearly loves his sister and would be the first to open his pockets to help her out because as anyone would attest his reputation for generosity knew no bounds. The only way that he could finance such a scheme would be to take out a loan. However he cannot take out a loan because the terms of the will expressly prohibited him from raising a brass farthing against the inheritance. If he were to do so, he claims, the trustees would become the sole beneficiaries of the entire estate leaving him without a penny. Thomas Jordan and his brother-in-law John Bradley who also works in the same trade are listening intently.

The trustees, he tells them, are devious, they have set a moneylender on him to tempt him with offers, he is in receipt of letters each day with the promise of all the money he would want and as proof he shows them typewritten letters purporting to come from a Mr King offering him sizeable sums of money. However he claims to know their game, the moneylender Mr King has only one interest and that was to entrap him and thus thwart his inheritance. He tells them that he is resolved to resist these offers with all his might.

Now both Mr Jordan and Mr Bradley start receiving telegrams directly from the money-lender, Mr King. In these messages Mr King suggests that if they should make a loan to Mr Burrell and have evidence that they have done so, they would be paid handsomely for their troubles. The telegrams meanwhile add weight to the veracity of Burrell's story and demonstrate the pressure of his predicament.

Each day from then on he went in to his work and lamented on the failing health of his sister and his own despair about the impotence of his position. Soon people were offering him money and even then Burrell refused help. He presented a circular argument with a peculiar logic of its own. He could not take their money because he was unable to offer them the security of any written confirmation of such a loan, without which their investment would be at risk. However, if he offered them a written agreement, which is the least he should do as a gentleman and details of the loan became known to the trustees, then as he had claimed, his inheritance would be null and void. At the same time any hope of their loan being repaid would also be lost. He could not countenance risking their money so recklessly. Therefore he could see no remedy without an agreement but he was grateful to know that he had such true friends.

The solution to his problem came a few days later. Thomas Jordan offered him two hundred pounds, a sizeable sum, more than enough to cover the cost of a sea cruise. More importantly, he offered to loan the money on the quiet without the necessity of a paper record. It would be a gentleman's agreement made on a handshake. Burrell again was reticent, he argued that although he was a trusting soul at heart and if the tables were turned at this juncture he would be the first to offer to help, he could not ask someone else to subscribe to such a risk. He made it very plain that they both could lose everything in such an enterprise. However Mr Jordan was set in his course and pressed the money upon Burrell. Soon others were offering sums including Mr Bradley.

It was some weeks later that Mr Jordan approached the police reporting he was concerned that Mr Henry Burrell had failed to attend his work.

Burrell, it transpired, had subsequently changed his employment and moved with his wife and child to a house in the grounds of the Asylum at St Albans, where Burrell was employed as a porter. When we arrived at the house, all the clothes were packed and gone although the heavier items of furniture were still there. In amongst various discarded papers I located a receipt from a shipping agent in Pall Mall. Conversation with his present employers indicated that the Burrells had not been seen for several days but significantly one neighbour in the asylum grounds had witnessed them leaving with a large amount of luggage in a hansom cab before dawn a couple of days earlier.

My next call was to the shipping agents in Pall Mall. I spoke to a clerk, who recognised the receipt and said he had sold passage to Sydney, Australia to a gentleman for two passengers in third class. The gentleman matched the description of Henry Burrell but the names on the tickets did not. It seemed that he had taken an alias as these passengers were a Henry and Lily Barker. He advised me that the boat had already sailed from Southampton the day before.

I spoke to Mr Jordan and said that from our enquiries it seemed most likely that Mr Henry Burrell and his wife had left the country for Australia but he had taken an assumed name. Could he think of any reason why Mr Burrell would do that? Mr Jordan then revealed the whole story about the unusual inheritance and the money that he and his brother-in-law had loaned to Mr Burrell. Poor Mr Jordan was stricken by the thought that he and his brother-in-law had given over their life savings to someone that they now realised they did not know at all. The cunning of this scheme was that there was no paperwork to speak of. Despite this we would have to ascertain whether there was any veracity in the claims.

The Thetford police made enquiries at the factory of Charles Burrell. They confirmed there was no family member called Henry Burrell. So he was a fraud and this was no short term impersonation as he had been living as Henry Burrell for well over eighteen months. The question of who he really was would have to wait, because every hour he was steaming further away from justice. Our advantage was that we knew the vessel he was sailing on, its direction of travel and its final destination.

I began to wonder if it would be possible to get a message to the next port of call. By this time it had already left Madeira but by using the science of telegraphy we were able to send a message around the world to South Africa where the boat was scheduled to land about a week later. We asked the South African Police to arrest Harry Barker or Henry Burrell and his wife Lily and send them back to face prosecution in Britain. They were arrested on the dockside in Cape Town on the 4th of June. It was found that they had upgraded their tickets from third class to first class on the boat. They would receive no such luxury on their return journey to justice at the expense of the British taxpayer.

It was nearly eight weeks after their arrest in Cape Town that Henry Burrell and his wife Lily were taken into custody at Paddington police station. I was a detective sergeant at the time but I was asked to interview the man known as Henry Burrell or Harry Barker with my colleague Inspector Pollard. The prisoner arrived full of energy and bluster claiming that he was Henry Burrell and that his inheritance was from his Aunt, a late Mrs Holland of Errieswell Court, near Thetford in Norfolk. He named a Mr Mouchin, a solicitor in Thetford as a trustee of the will. When questioned about his alias, Harry Barker, he claimed that he felt it prudent under the circumstances not to be seen spending money in his own name lest it come to the attention of the trustees of the will. When questioned about his disappearance which had caused the alarm to be raised, he said that the trustees had been closing in on him and he felt it better to avoid them by going abroad until his inheritance was proved. He was sorry that this should have caused consternation to Mr Jordan and Mr Bradley but he had to leave without giving any indication of where he was going lest others who bore him nothing but ill-will should find him. As events proved this young man certainly had some gumption but if he thought he was going to be set free without further enquiry he was to be sorely disappointed.

Next Inspector Pollard and I interviewed Lily Burrell. A pretty young girl with fair hair and a pleasant face. From the start she was much more willing to co-operate with our enquiries. I began by asking how she had met Mr Burrell and she told of him coming into her public house and wooing her from the start. She said that although at first he was a kind and attentive man, he was stricken with moods. Sometimes he could be the most charming man in the world, full of vim and verve and at other times he would be down in the dumps and inconsolable with melancholy. I asked her to tell me more about these changes and what might have brought them about. She said that he would often stay out late at night without reason and once she was so alarmed by his erratic comings and goings that she went through his belongings. This was when she came across a marriage certificate but the names on it made no sense. It was, she said a marriage certificate for a Mr Harry Bensley to a Miss Kate

Green. The marriage took place in 1898, in Thetford. That evening when Burrell returned home Mrs Burrell confronted him with the evidence.

At first he denied that he was Harry Bensley, claiming to have no knowledge of him but Mrs Burrell was not to be persuaded and demanded, 'If that is the case why do you have this certificate? It is obvious to me that you are this Harry Bensley.'

He then conceded that yes, this certificate would suggest that he was Harry Bensley. Furthermore, the event that it pertains to did indeed happen but he claimed it was not a real marriage. This Kate Green, the bride, was a daughter of a dear friend of his Aunt, she had been unfortunate in love and had asked for help to keep her respectable. Being a gentleman and old friend of the family and of course wishing to save her reputation, Burrell then told Lily that he had arranged a short ceremony and the manufacture of the false certificate so that Miss Green could say that she was married. He also alleged that he had arranged the notification of the death of her 'husband' to the local press. In this way her reputation could be saved as Miss Green could claim to be a widower and not have a child out of wedlock. He then apologised for the distress to his wife and said he should have destroyed the document years ago.

However, later that very evening he came over with the melancholy and Lily found him lying on the floor of their bathroom with an empty bottle of laudanum beside him. Quickly she administered mustard and water to him and he slowly recovered but she revealed to me that she believed that he meant to take his life.

Finally Lily disclosed an even more puzzling event. He asked Lily to write a letter at his dictation in the name of Mrs Henrietta Moncrieff and to send the letter to Mrs Kate Bensley at her last known address. We will hear more of the contents of this letter later.

The fact of the marriage was quickly verified, the registry of births, deaths and marriages has a complete record of a Harry Bensley marrying a Kate Green. Now there was no doubt of his real name.

At the next interview, Lily Clapham as we must now call her is full of regret for the flight from Britain and it is obvious that she was as much a victim in this fraud as those who had lost money. In many ways she lost much more. The charge of her being an accomplice was dropped on condition that she gave evidence at any trial, to which she readily agreed and was therefore set free.

Harry Bensley as we now knew him to be was a harder nut to crack. He held by his story that he was Henry Burrell but the evidence against him was growing by the day. More people were coming forward saying they had made him a loan but the major amounts were three hundred pounds from Thomas Jordan and sixty-seven pounds from John Bradley. Tidy sums and it should be noted most of it had been spent on board the ship.

We questioned him further about his aliases. The first thing to notice is that his initials were the same, whether Barker, Burrell or Bensley it was always HB. Whether he had learnt this trick or had used raw cunning was difficult to tell. One stroke of good fortune for the police was finding Harry Bensley's name in the criminal record system and we now knew that he had served time for stealing money and theft of clothes. At this point he admitted that he was Harry Bensley and we were then ready to take him to Willesden Magistrates Court and charge him with obtaining money under false pretences. The Magistrate remanded Bensley in custody.

The Courtroom was full of members of the press. They dubbed him the 'Bogus Heir' as the story of him posing as the son of a famous engineering company was hot news. This coupled with his failed attempt to escape justice made it a very popular story.

Every court case requires the diligent legwork of the police and we had to provide evidence of the untruths of his claimed heirdom, which was a complicated story. However it was made simple by outright denials of the existence of the Aunt, or the will, or any such legacy by the solicitors involved. The evidence of the money being taken from Mr Jordan and Mr Bradley was sworn on oath. Finally, we gathered evidence of his flight from Britain.

While Harry Bensley was remanded into custody we were engaged with collecting evidence for the trial. Our main concern was the fraud and deception charge, because there were so many loose ends that it would be possible for a skilled advocate to tie witnesses in knots around the conflicting evidence. The other problem that we were anticipating was, what if he denied taking the money from Mr Jordan and Mr Bradley, or claimed it was a gift? The cunning of his original plan was that this was a possible defence, where it would be one person's word against another's. For many a skilled barrister there is less than a hair's breadth between fraud and a legal defence and they could make merry with the finer details.

I interviewed Harry Bensley again and this time he was reserved and melancholic. I asked him to tell me about his first marriage. He said that Kate Green was his childhood sweetheart, that they had met when he was only fourteen and had been friends for years until they married in 1898. They had two children and moved to London and then she deserted him. He still loved her though, even saying that his wife was still the lodestone of his life. He claimed that none of this would have happened if his wife had not deserted him because it had put him in a disturbed state of mind. So much so that the day when he walked in to the Duke of Clarence and set eyes upon Miss Lily Clapham, he fell in love at first sight or at least he thought he did and made up this story as a way to woo her. Once he had started lying the stories just continued and he was unable to find an escape. Months later he realised too late that he had lost Kate, the love of his life and that was when he tried to commit suicide. When this was unsuccessful, he did attempt to get back in contact with his wife by sending a letter to her last known address but she failed to reply. Accepting that it was all over and there was no chance of a reconciliation he decided to start afresh on a different continent but being arrested was the best thing for him, as it was a great relief to stop the lying.

I asked him if he had divorced and he said no. I told him that without a divorce he would be regarded as married whatever the circumstances and that a bigamy charge was a foregone conclusion. He refused to understand the very straightforward nature of the offence and clung to his belief that his wife had deserted him.

After this interview I made the journey to Thetford and met with his wife, Kate Bensley. She was a respectable hard working woman, by now employed as a housekeeper for the family of a doctor. She was aware that her husband had taken up with another woman and told me that her circumstances at the time meant that she had been forced to sell up all her goods and apply to the poor house. Fortunately a good friend in Thetford came forward and offered her work so she could return to her home town. She was using her maiden name of Green which made me speculate whether it was possible that she had taken out divorce proceedings against Bensley without his knowledge. Mrs Bensley said she had neither the resources nor the inclination to divorce, indeed she went further and stated that she still loved her husband or at least the memory of him despite all that had happened.

We had the evidence required to win the bigamy case. I told Mrs Bensley that she should be prepared to be called as a witness and she said that she was ready to do it but if it would be possible to avoid having to give evidence in court she would be much obliged, as she would 'maybe have the faints in such a rare atmosphere'. She said that she would make the journey to attend the trial to see her husband, and asked that I keep her informed of the date and the venue so that she could make arrangements to travel.

Bensley was taken back to Willesden Police Court and remanded on the charge of bigamy.

I went to the previous address of Mrs Kate Bensley in South Norwood and met a Mrs Rose Smith, the landlady. Mrs Smith confirmed that Mrs Bensley lived there for several months after the breakdown of their marriage. I asked her about this letter that Lily Burrell claimed she wrote under dictation to this address and Mrs Smith confirmed that she had received it. Better still, she still had a copy of it.

This is a transcript of the contents that I noted at the time:

Dear Madam,

Would you kindly write to me to the address enclosed as you might hear something to your advantage. Please enclose your address and if your name was Kate Green. Also if you was in an orphanage at Ipswich and if you have any children, their names and ages. Would you kindly answer this by return as I am only making a short stay and oblige,

Yours truly,

Mrs Henrietta Moncrieff.

Mrs Smith went on to tell me that over a year later Harry Bensley knocked on her door and asked if his wife was there. She said no, he then asked her if she knew where his wife was and she said no. Bensley said he had heard that his wife was expecting another child and that he wanted to find his children. Mrs Smith told him about the letter from Mrs Moncrieff and that she had not answered it. Bensley said she ought to have done so and she would have been well paid for her trouble. Mrs Smith asked Bensley who Mrs Moncrieff was but he did not tell her and then he went away.

The trial took place in front of the Common Serjeant Sir Frederick Bosanquet, one of the most senior and respected judges at the Old Bailey. The modern oak panelled court was packed out with reporters and members of the public in the spectators' gallery. Their main interest was the tale of the bogus heir, so there was general disappointment when Bensley, who had decided to defend himself, pleaded guilty to that charge, as that would mean the juicy details of the whole affair would not be aired in the court room. However there was an audible gasp of surprise when he said, 'Not guilty' to the charge of bigamy. Even his first wife, who was sitting amongst the members of the public in full view of Harry Bensley, was visibly shocked. Although we had some inkling that this was going to be his plea, we had hoped that the full majesty of the law court would cause a change of heart in the defendant.

The prosecuting counsel had prepared diligently and was ready to present the case. First on the stand was Lily Mosby, who was one of the witnesses to the wedding between the defendant and Miss Kate Green. She gave a good account of herself and showed the marriage certificate to the court. There was no doubt in the mind of the jury of the event of the first marriage.

The next witness was the landlady, Mrs Rose Smith. She gave evidence as to the breakdown of the marriage, and Mrs Bensley having continued to live in the South Norwood house for nearly fifteen months after Bensley had left. She also told of the strange affair of the letter from Mrs Henrietta Moncrieff and Harry Bensley's visit to the house a year later. This stirred the defendant and he decided to cross examine Mrs Smith. He asked her to say where his wife had gone after leaving the house and Mrs Smith said she had left to go to the poor house. This piece of information seemed to catch Bensley off balance.

Next to give evidence was Lily Clapham. She may once have been beautiful but by now she was a thin shadow as she took the stand and recounted her tale of woe for the prosecution. There were further details of her being kept away from her family and friends. Even letters that she was sending out for possible employment were intercepted or never sent by Bensley. He was pictured as a very unstable and deeply controlling individual. Despite her many undoubted misgivings she had continued to stay at his side until their arrest in Cape Town.

Bensley again cross examined the witness who was brave in the face of his challenge. He asked if it were true that she did not receive any communications. She said that she did receive one letter after all but this was in reply to a letter that she had posted herself, thereby avoiding the censorious Bensley. His other questions only elicited responses that worsened his case. Miss Clapham claimed the only reason they married was so that she might go to Queen Charlotte Hospital to give birth. Then she stated that Bensley tried to manipulate her by saying he would commit suicide unless she went along with his schemes and strategies and on one occasion he actually did try, or so he had claimed. That little detail was maybe the most damning comment of all. A small moment of public triumph after two disastrous years for Miss Clapham.

This had taken up until midday and the prosecution rested their case. Sir Frederick called a recess and as I left the courtroom I was met by the court beadle who asked that I visit the prisoner in the cells below. I found Bensley in a state of wild panic, wailing and bemoaning his predicament. A witness he was relying upon to make his case for desertion had with a certain delicious irony, deserted him. He reminded me that I had interviewed this man, a Mr Burton and required him to be there. He then begged me to take the stand but I was perplexed. What possible good could come of my evidence? My interview with Mr Burton was of such little consequence with no proper facts I had barely made note of it. I said in any case if he called me as a witness I was obliged to take the stand. This calmed him down to the extent that he could sit but he would not eat. The only thing that gave him cheer he said, was seeing his wife in the public gallery. I helped him take some water and sat silently with him as a kindness until the afternoon's proceedings were ready to commence.

The court beadle asked us to rise and Sir Frederick asked the prisoner to offer his defence. They called out my name and it is one of the very few occasions where I have been asked to give evidence on behalf of the defence.

Harry Bensley started by asking if I had met a Mr Burton and under what circumstances. I replied 'I have been to see a Mr Burton and I warned him to be here to give evidence.'

'What did Mr Burton show you at that meeting?'

'Mr Burton showed me a letter that he had received from you, asking him to give evidence to the effect that he went with you to where your first wife had been living and that when you got there you found that your home had been sold up.'

As I answered this question Harry Bensley only had eyes for his wife. He was watching her intently to see what her reaction would be. Mrs Kate Bensley was gazing back. Her demeanour was more animated, she was more alive than I had seen her before and there was something charged in the air between them. Then Bensley realised I had stopped speaking and tried to formulate another question, the answer to which I doubt was helpful to his cause.

'I have made inquiries and find that your first wife, you having left her, heard something about a second wife and sold the home to provide herself with means of living.'

He thanked me and asked me to leave the stand. Finally it was Harry Bensley's turn to speak. He took the stand and swore the oath before giving his curious defence.

'If a man is like a ship then when I walked out on my wife it was as if the cables that held down the cargo in the hold had come loose, and my mind yawed violently from one course to another. Frankly I was lost without her and although I came back to my senses and with Mr Burton we did go back to our last address but sadly we were too late. On realising that my entire family had disappeared my inner compass spun recklessly once again. I fell completely in love with Miss Clapham at first sight when I was at this difficult point in my life. I walked out with her for a while and then we agreed that I should meet with her father. He took against me almost immediately as he did not think I was a suitable person to be with his daughter. He created a scene so distressing that afterwards in consequence Miss Clapham said she could no longer return to her home. She asked me to find her somewhere to live. For a while we lived together and I continued to try and find my first wife without success. Eventually I married Miss Clapham but did not think I was doing wrong because I had made every effort to find my first wife.'

The prosecution made no cross-examination of the prisoner and the presentation of evidence was completed. The jury were asked to give their verdict but the instruction from the Common Serjeant was clear. 'Marriage is a union of one man and one woman in law for life. There are duties and obligations to each other and the community at large that come from that union. Without a legal divorce the marriage still stands in law and any further marriage can only be classed as bigamy regardless of the circumstances that bring it about. The prosecution has shown evidence of the marriage. The defence has presented a peculiar story of desertion but no evidence of any divorce. For you, the members of the jury, this is a very straightforward case.'

The jury came back into the court room within twenty minutes and there was no doubt about the verdict. Guilty.

Sir Frederick then considered the matter of the sentence. These were two serious charges. The fraud was on a large scale and had caused much misery and suffering not to mention the cost to the public purse of returning him to justice. Then there was the bigamy that had also caused enormous suffering to two innocent women. There was also his previous criminal record, in which the punishment he had received showed no sign of rehabilitating this offender. Under these circumstances he was to be sentenced to four years penal servitude on each indictment, to run concurrently.

The wild panic I saw in the cells was gone. Bensley stood taller and prouder than at any time during the court case and once the Common Serjeant had finished his sentencing he said the most remarkable thing.

'Thank you my Lord, I have deserved it.'

Postscript

There are many who would say lock him up and throw away the key as Bensley was obviously a bad seed and by now a career criminal. I would ask them to read this postscript.

I met Harry Bensley nearly thirty years later at a police function in Colchester town hall in the county of Essex. As Chief Inspector of the Metropolitan Police I had been asked to present certain prizes to worthy citizens at a civic event. In the formal introduction line at the beginning of the evening I was introduced to Councillor and Mrs Bensley. I recognised him immediately and to my surprise he was smiling broadly and shook my hand with great warmth. Later that evening he told me that his trial was the turning point in his life and he thanked me for the small kindness I had shown him when he was in his cell at the Old Bailey. Thirty years later and he had been of good character, was reconciled with his wife and family and never troubled the law courts again. He was now a local councillor for Wivenhoe, a small port near Colchester. I watched him that evening, holding hands with his wife Kate. They were obviously very happy together. It was one of the rare occasions that I was to witness the fruits of rehabilitation from the firm but fair application of the criminal justice system.

PART 3

Truth, be told

Kate's kitchen – 1

Thetford, November 1908

'I can't see how to start this Kate, I mean how do I begin?'

'Well, let's see what to call it. Maybe 'whatever happened to the Man in the Mask?' I suppose the best place to start is to tell them about the time you were in gaol.'

'But I can't go into the details because someone might be able to work out who I really am.'

'No, you can't do that but maybe you could say what you said to the judge at the end of the trial.'

'Really, you think so?'

'I think everyone was struck by it, I know that when you said it, it was what gave me hope.'

'So what happened again, the judge sentences me to penal servitude...'

'And you say...'

'...Thank you my Lord, I deserve it!'

'That's good, write that down, it's a strong start, that would get my attention.'

'What next Kate? I suppose I'd better speak about prison.'

'Let's start there and see where it goes.'

Junk

Pentonville, 1905

Pick, pick, pick with your fingers.

At least I can't smell it any more but my fingers are burning, I mustn't cry out or they'll put me on the frame as they did to that little weasel-faced blagger in front of me. I can see the welts forming on the back of his neck and he's simpering like a baby.

This junk's nasty today, the tar's so stiff because of the cold and I can hardly get it on my spike, there's no way I'll get my dinner with this rubbish. The windows are rattling with the wind which does at least mean that I can feel fresh air even if I can't taste it.

Pick, pick, pick with your fingers.

What's that noise? Don't look up. Just because I heard something, mustn't look up, the screws are always provoking for someone who looks up. I'll take a sideways glance while I move my stick of junk.

I can't see anything special. Just all of us with our heads down and the screws pacing hard like farm dogs craftily circling a herd of sheep. The silence is empty, except for the whistle of the wind, the scratch of junk and the echo of heel on floorboard. It makes the voice in your head sing out loud, until you can't quieten it any longer.

I can hear shouts. Don't look up, don't look up. What can I hear? The cries don't make sense. Footsteps, people running from all directions. There's a scuffle erupting, the screws are piling in. The sounds are muffled but I can hear a stick landing on soft flesh.

What's this giant of a fellow next to me up to? He's smiling my way and looking at me, isn't he alive to the peril? He is glancing down at his hand, which is moving near. There's a scrap of paper in it. He's looking at me, he wants me to take it. If I move my hand and reposition the junk I can take the paper but what am I going to do with it now? I don't have a pocket and my fingers are all gummy from the nasty junk.

I make as if my back is in pain and move my hand to the back of my neck, then down inside my tunic and get some tar on my spine, now firmly press the note against my back. There, the note is stuck to my body. Don't look back at him. Just a little hidden thumbs up while I tease up the locks of junk.

Pick, pick, pick with your fingers.

I can just see him at the edge of my eye. Everyone knows of him because he is startlingly large, some say he's a German, I've never heard him speak though. Nothing unusual in that, in fact I could say I've never heard voice from most of the people here. It is those that you hear speaking that get in the deepest water. I don't want trouble, I just want to get through each day and back to my cell. He's made a thumbs up too. Interesting.

The Chaplain strides in. He tells us that the devil walks amongst us, stirring up passions so we must turn to Christ to make our thoughts pure because the only road to repentance is through Christ our Lord. The bulky prisoner next to me is shuffling around, I can spy his hand and he makes a thumbs up again. Strange. I glance to his face, a dangerous thing to do if I am spotted but the Chaplain is looking away from us and most of the screws are still busy. This fellow's rugged face has a hint of a smile again, just enough for me to see.

Stop picking.

Stand up, don't talk, hold the rope and march single file to the cells. The big man is in front of me blocking the view, he walks with a strong gait and is still well built for a man who has spent a long time in prison. The clothes hang off most of us prisoners but he fills his tunic out like a barrel of muscle. Stop at the door, walk through the exercise yard. Exercise yard! They take us out of our cells and make us walk around and around on Sundays but for a few moments it is good to taste fresh air after the eye-burning stench of the tar in the oakum shed. Only a few steps and a couple of deep breaths of clean air then back inside the main prison. There's another line of prisoners coming in from the other side of the main building from the sawmill. We stop and stand and stare at each other, those whose minds are crumbling from tedium and those whose bodies are slumped from exhaustion. What is worse? It doesn't matter, it's all bad.

A gaoler brings the keys and opens the gate to the stairs, up we go, the mindless workers trudge to the next level, I turn off here for my cell and the big fellow leads the way, his vast body filling the gangway. We walk along, he stops at a cell door, the one before mine. He's my neighbour and I didn't even know it. Perhaps that is new, I am sure I would remember him. The gaoler opens his door and lets him in, he then shuts and locks the door. Next it is my turn, I go into my cell and listen for the closing of the lock behind me, now at last it is time to find out what is on the note that I can still feel stuck to my spine.

Come to the window, farmer boy.

The window is high at the end of the cell. I stand on my hard board bed and can just see the sky and strangely distant on the wind I can hear his voice. He has a very gentle accent, surprising for such a giant of a man, whose voice if it had matched his body would shake the whole prison.

The wind outside breathed softly and then roared, muffling and fluttering the words around the cell walls as he announced himself as Torben Maier. He had come from a small farming village near Tegernsee in Southern Bavaria, a beautiful place he said, a large clear blue water lake surrounded by mountains. He had heard me sing of being a farmer boy, which was true as I would sometimes of an evening cheer myself with a verse or two of an old work song from home. He continued, saying that as a youngster he would help on the family farm with the cows, taking them to pasture and gathering hay but he said there was no possibility of work when he was older as his older brothers were to work on the farm and there was not enough land for the three of them. Because he had excelled in mathematics at school and he had learned good English, he was told by a relative that work could be found in England. Good honest work that would set him up for a career in administration back in Bavaria.

So that's how he came here and became a clerk working in book-keeping. 'But you,' he says, 'you're a farmer boy. Where are you from and what are you doing in London?'

So I tell him I'm from Norfolk, which he's never heard of and yes I was a farmer's boy but that was years ago. I do love to sing the songs though and that was how I met my first love.

'Are you still together?' he asks.

'No, that is my greatest regret,' I say, 'because when we were together everything made sense but now nothing does.'

'Nothing does.' He repeats quietly and then he says, 'Sing me a song farmer boy, your voice reminds me of home'.

So I do...

The sun had set, beneath the hill, beyond the dreary moor,
when weary and lame, a poor boy came, up to a farmer's door
saying 'Can you tell me, if any there be, that can give me employ,
To plough and to sow and reap and to mow, and be a farmer's boy,
and be a farmer's boy.

...and as I sang I could hear on the wind my German neighbour humming a beautiful harmony.

'Good night, farmer boy.'

'Good night, Torben.'

Resurrection

Pentonville, 1905

'Let's sing a hymn, farmer boy.'

That's a strange request and no mistake. After a long day's work in the oakum shed my German neighbour wants to sing a hymn. I've had enough of hymns, if it isn't sermons of hard work and redemption it's hymns. All the time in the chapel we sing to the glory of God. I don't raise my voice for a hymn, I need all my energy to get through the day.

'Come on, farmer boy, let sing a hymn.'

I don't want to sing a hymn Torben, besides it reminds me of Kate. Hymns are from the good times and there's precious few of them in here. If I sing a hymn it will taint the memories and I need those memories to be remain pure.

'I have a plan farmer boy but you and I, we, we need to sing a hymn and we need to sing it together. I don't know the words because we didn't sing your little English hymns in my Bavarian Church but you can help me to know it and farmer boy, we need to learn something that will be sung in the chapel pretty soon, because you and I want to stand out.'

I never sing in the chapel. Instead I mumble and pretend I can't make the notes but for some reason I will humour Torben. Let's think of a hymn, Easter is approaching, so maybe 'When I survey the wondrous cross' would be a good choice. It's got a melody, something we could work with and I know most of the words to the first verse at least.

'Sing it for me.'

I do and I can feel Torben listening hard. 'It is a typical dull English tune with none of the majesty of Mozart or Beethoven.'

Do you want me to choose another? Then he says he thinks he can make a counter melody and perhaps we can carry the day in the chapel.

'Sing it again.'

I can hear him trying out harmonies.

'Once more, keep going.'

We carry on, his strong counter melody dipping under and flying over my voice, sometimes keeping quiet at other times bellowing forth.

'Stop. How many verses has it got?'

I don't know and why should I? I've never counted the verses. It's a short hymn though.

'Short is good, we can do the main melody on the first verse, then I'll counter low and quiet in the middle and on the final verse, I'll counter high and loud. You have to work with me, we have to grab their attention from the start and stand out from the rest. We practice each day until we get it right and then we keep it up so we are ready for Chapel.'

What's the point of this? I mean I used to enjoy a sing-song don't get me wrong but I sing about things that make me smile and laugh. Chapel singing does nothing for me. At least it isn't hard labour for the body but it might as well be hard labour for the mind. Torben is insistent though. He said that my problem was that I couldn't wait to put a plan in action but act on impulse.

'Don't trust impulse' he said. 'Impulse has not been your friend.'

Every day he would keep up his campaign to practice and be ready for the moment we sing the hymn in Chapel. He told me to continue to mumble the hymns until then.

On Sundays we would be led out of our cells. It was fortunate that he was such a size, because it was easy to spot him as he resembled a mountain top above the clouds of prisoners in the exercise yard. If we could, we would move together before being herded into the Chapel for Service. The hymn books were handed to us on the way in and the hymn numbers displayed on a wooden noticeboard beside the Cross carved by the prisoners that was mounted on the wall behind the Chaplain.

Then one Sunday there it was, the last hymn. I couldn't see Torben because of the screens that were installed between each of the prisoners so we could not look at each other. I could hear someone shuffling their feet about, making the loudest shuffle I've ever heard and I knew that meant Torben had seen the hymn number as well. I could feel butterflies fluttering in my stomach even though I had the easy part, to sing the hymn as was but in my best and loudest voice. It was Torben who was going to make the biggest impact by harmonising. What would they do? This could turn out very bad. They could put us in isolation. They could strap us to the whipping frame. Why were we doing this stupid thing? Keep your head down, don't get noticed, that's how to get through this.

The organ has started playing the first chords so here we go. All I can hear is Torben and my voice. The Chaplain has a puzzled look on his face, now he is looking up he is looking around, now he is looking our way, he's looking, I'm not sure I've seen that look before, bemused, I suppose. He doesn't normally get such a rousing rendition from the prisoners. Second verse, I'm taking the lead and Torben's ducking under, it's coming together quite beautifully. Look in the hymnal, there's four verses. Third verse, Torben has lifted the volume a bit, I'm keeping it steady as we go, the rest of the prisoners have stopped singing, it's just us. Final verse, full volume from both of us and Torben's counter high notes are getting wide-eyed looks from the Chaplain.

The Service is over and the Chaplain is staring at us. There is a murmur amongst the rest of the prisoners as they file out. Some of the prisoners that I glimpse are looking strangely at me. What's my game, what am I doing? The Chaplain meanwhile makes eye contact with two of the warders and points at us. 'I want them to stay' he says. Once the other prisoners are outside we are led down to the front of the Chapel.

The Chaplain's face gave nothing away and his voice was neutral in tone.

'Whose idea was this?'

I was glad that Torben made to answer the question as I was struggling to think of anything to say but Torben replied that he had heard me singing in my cell and was convinced that everyone should have the opportunity to hear my pure voice. The Chaplain turned to me.

'You've never sung in Chapel before' he stated.

No, I hadn't, I had never wanted to but Torben convinced me by singing harmonious melodies.

'Why did you do it?'

Torben replied saying we both enjoyed singing and wanted to show everyone how we could praise the Lord. The Chaplain looked intently at us both, weighing our answers.

'You' he said looking at Torben, 'You're not English, are you? What is your name and why are you here?'

Torben stood looking into the distance impassively without complaint, his voice hushed and precise.

'My name is Torben Maier and I am from Bavaria and I am here because I sinned when I stole money from my employer.'

'And you?'

'My name is Harry Bensley and I sinned when I committed fraud and bigamy.'

He nodded, taking in what he had heard, then he walked slowly about the front of the chapel with his head in thought.

'I will look into this matter. Let them go.'

Thirst

'Stop. Quiet, quiet. Back to the beginning of the verse. Kesby, play the main tune from the beginning and listen tenors when you sing, 'In every way He faithful will remain,' I want to hear much more emphasis on the 'He' and it's a semitone higher on the 'remain'. Now, keep to time, watch my baton, sprightly, now. One, two, three...'

Who would believe that singing is hard work but that's what it is. It's easier than picking junk but it's no simple option. The Chaplain wants us to sing louder and longer and we all keep going until we fair lose our voice because our mouths are dry and our throats are on fire.

The Chaplain stops the music again.

'What's wrong with you? Come on, sprightly I say, raise up your voices.'

'We can't, sir.'

'What did you say Maier?'

'We can't, sir. We are unused to using our voices so strongly and we are thirsty from all the singing.'

'You are right, we shall need some refreshment. I should have thought of that. Thank you Maier for being so bold as to tell me what is wrong.'

He left the Chapel and for the first time we could talk. Torben looked around at the rest of us. Held his finger to his mouth and bade us to be quiet.

'This is better than the sawmill or picking oakum? Yes?' He whispered.

We all nodded.

'We must make him think we need more practice, so we get better, yes, but not so much better. If he wants his choir to be ready for his fancy concert then he needs to spend more time with us.'

Again we all nodded in agreement. Any plan that involved less hard labour was a good plan.

'We need to make one or two things to go wrong but never the same person or he will think they are bad and take them from the choir. So, I will look your way before the start of each piece and you make a mistake. A wrong note, or hold a note too long, then next time you get it right but I look to someone else for a mistake. This way he will think it is necessary for more rehearsal during work time so we are not so tired to sing.'

I had to admire Torben. From hearing me sing to the formation of a prison choir, this had all been his idea and we were all benefitting from the arrangement. In two week's time we were to give a concert to an audience of the Society for the Promotion of Christian Knowledge as an example of the results of the work of spreading the word of the Lord amongst the prisoners. My personal benefit was six afternoons away from the hated oakum shed. Others were taken from the sawmill and some even had time off from solitary and the dreaded hand-crank. If there were more ways of escaping the hours of tedium, we were all for it.

The Chaplain returned followed by a warder who had brought a carboy of water on a trolley with some stone mugs and we quenched our thirst. Torben looked around at the crowd and nodded towards a young lad. He glanced back and acknowledged that it was his turn to make the error. The Chaplain ended the break, tapped his baton on the piano, then stood poised with both arms up. Kesby played the prelude and we prepared to sing again. The boy's first note was loud and raucous, bringing the hymn to a grinding halt before it even got started. Everybody stopped and laughed, while the boy held his mouth as if it is was this organ that had deliberately caused the offence.

'Sorry, too much water,' he apologised. Torben flashed an angry look his way before tapping me on my hand. I can do this, one slightly duff high note is all it needs and I can deliver that very easily. The rest of the practice comes together and Torben slows down the deliberate mistakes. The Chaplain can hear us improving but there is still work to be done.

Torben and I are held back by the Chaplain at the end of the practice.

'I can't help but notice Maier, that the other prisoners look up to you and from what I have witnessed you are a good influence and they take a lead from you. Bensley, your voice is the best in the choir and your behaviour is always an example to the other prisoners. You have both shown yourselves to be ideal candidates to demonstrate the improvement that comes from the work of the Society for the Promotion of Christian Knowledge. We have been preparing a new scheme. The Governor has granted me permission to reopen the library and we will need honest Christian staff to administer it. I am putting your names forward with my recommendation and heartfelt approval. It will require you to work in the evenings but I am sure that you will benefit from the access to improving books.'

Library

Pentonville, 1906

'What do you have there, farmer boy?'

'New books, Torben, new books from the Chaplain. Some are even in reasonable condition and one or two are actual books, not the usual scripture lessons. I'll have to bind the spines on these though as some of the pages are loose.'

'We need more card and glue, it is all run out. Does nobody look after books in England? They are never in good condition. I will talk to the Chaplain about new supplies. Did you fill the book truck, farmer boy? I will take it on B-wing tonight. And have you seen the ledger book? I know there are many books on loan along there and it is time to call them in.'

'You have that skill down to an art, Torben. I think that many of the prisoners quake when the "Ox" looms by.'

'The Ox, is that what they call me? I'm not a physical man, despite my size. All I do is ask and they return the books. After all the Chaplain has more power of punishment than I.'

'My words don't weigh so heavily as yours when it's my turn to collect the books.'

Torben smiled and started to rearrange the books on the shelves of the truck. He glanced at the table in the library.

'What are you writing, farmer boy?'

'A letter, a letter to my wife, to give her my news about working in the library and hope to hear something of hers. How she is coping, how my children are growing up. It would give me the most joy if she was to visit but it is a long way to travel and very expensive.'

'She does not write to you?'

'She writes short notes thanking me for my letters but no more. I despair of what it can mean because she gives me no sign.'

'You should not despair. Why do you not ask her what she means?'

'In my head I can already hear what she would say and it scares me to hear it. So that I may find the stamina to keep going until the end of my sentence, I need to have some hope, even if it is of my own manufacture, so I would rather not hear her truth lest it take that hope away from me.'

'The voice in your head, it does not know your Kate as you think but you can get answers without asking questions.'

'What do you mean?'

'Why do you think she writes back to you at all?'

'To acknowledge my letters.'

'But think farmer boy, why is that important to her?'

'I don't know, I wish I knew but I don't.'

'I think she would not write back, if there was not some hope for you.'

'You think so?'

'Of course. Why would she? If she has another plan why keep writing back to you. She is not a schemer, not from what you told me. She is an open person without malice. You should tell her of your plans, what you are going to do when you leave.'

'I don't have a plan, Torben. I only have today.'

'And that is why you fail. You never have a plan. You act on impulse, you need to stop that, calm down and think of a future.'

'If only I could but the thoughts race fast in my head as if they are dogs coursing a hare and I lose all control, then I fall into despair.'

'I have heard of a thing such as this, a mania, I think it is called.'

'I don't care what it is called.'

'No but it is interesting, yes? I've seen it in you now, the enthusiasm and then the stillness. I need to tell you something farmer boy and this is very important. When we come to prison they take away our dignity with the shorn head and the scratching clothes. They exhaust our bodies with hard labour and tedious work. They dull our taste buds with vile food. They try and break into our thoughts with all the Christian teachings but there is one thing they cannot stop, they cannot stop us dreaming. At night we can escape. In here, in our minds we can still be free. You need to remember, in your mind you are still a free man.'

He paused and stood up and walked slowly about the library.

'I cannot tell you what you need to do but I think you should make a plan, because when you can see the way ahead, everything becomes clearer. Look at how I took the opportunity of your voice to bring us to the attention of the Chaplain. I was not sure of the outcome but it has led us both here, to a more comfortable existence. We are prisoners, yes but no more do we labour. We have status and a little power, I think. What you have to think of is the steps you need to take to win back your Kate. Think of them as small steps with a glorious goal.'

I still had no idea what to write in my letter but Torben was looking at me as if he had delivered wise words. He picked up some of the books that had just arrived and looked at the titles.

'Oh look at this, this old one is different. What is this, Dumas? The man in the iron mask? Oh, I remember, surely that is just part of the Vicomte de Bragelonne book isn't it? Those Musketeers, their final tragic adventure but what prisoner wants to read about another prisoner? That is a Christian joke isn't it? Never mind, I shall take it with me, there are some strange fellows out there.'

And with that he pushed the truck out onto the landing.

Plans

Pentonville, 1906

'One month to go, farmer boy, one month and I will be outside with fresh air in my lungs.'

Torben has kept saying his release date for weeks. I think he needs to keep reminding himself that there is not long to go. It is good for him but I have nearly a year before I will see my home and my wife. As his enthusiasm grows mine diminishes and it is strange to think of him not being here. He has been my friend and companion. A purveyor of hope amongst the despair. We sing in Chapel and we sing at concerts for prison visitors. The prize has been a reputation for being rehabilitated and the rewards, small but treasured have come to us. Working in the prison library is the biggest reward of all and now takes up all of our time.

I told him once again that I shall miss him and once more I asked about his plans and this time instead of just tapping his nose, he lent forward and whispered.

'My plans, farmer boy? I have several but one or two look more promising than others.'

'Tell me more.'

Torben looked around to see if anyone was about the library or on the landing outside.

'I told you I was a bookkeeper in an insurance company. There was one particular company that supplied stationery and typewriter machines. Paper, ink ribbon and carbon paper for typewriters mainly. They also had a contract to maintain the typewriters. The insurance company had a number of typewriters and supplies and maintenance was often needed. You would be surprised just what could go wrong with these machines, from losing a letter to the whole carriage flying away and because of this we frequently required their services. My immediate superior had the responsibility of ordering the stationery supplies among other things. I had to keep the accounts and every so often I would find some items missing from a delivery and then I would go to my superior and inform him. At first he would smooth it all over and make some excuse for the problem but paperwork would always be required to reconcile the accounts. Then one day he came and found me at a public bar after work.

'Torben,' he says, 'how are things going? Would an advance help you, if you could do some little thing for me?'

'I'm not a well-off person. The pay is low and they pay us Germans less than you English, which is not fair but work is work. I ask him how much the advance would be? A week's wages, he says. How often would I get this advance? Maybe every month or so depending on what was required and that is very tempting. So I ask what would I need to do to receive this advance? Just make some paperwork reconcile. The troublesome paperwork about the stationery supplies.'

Torben looked down, very sullen, sadder than I had ever seen him look.

'I didn't want to do it. I felt there was something, how do you English say, fishy about it but here was my superior offering me much money to make this happen. So it must be all right, yes? Next time the order comes in, I see that we are missing several boxes of paper that should have arrived. Rather than go to my superior, I alter the order to look as though the numbers are correct. A week or so later there is an order for two typewriters and only one is delivered. I do the same again and I think this is all good, I can make this work, this is what he wants me to do.'

'Of course what I forget to think about is why he wants me to do this. He is making the orders, he could check them and make good the discrepancies far better than I. So what is my role? That is what I did not think through, that is why I felt it was fishy.'

'After the typewriter delivery I was sure that I was due my advance but he kept avoiding me. When he did find me it was very unpleasant.

The director of the company came in to the workroom with him and asked to see the accounting books for the last two weeks but he also had carbon copies of the original orders and went through the ledgers one by one. It was only a matter of time before the mistakes was uncovered and what was more there was only one person who could have organised it and that was me. Then it became obvious that this had been going on for some time and I got all of the blame.'

'Us giants, people think we are slow of thought but in that moment I knew I would not be believed so I must take the consequence and stay quiet. Although I did not know why, not then but now my time is coming farmer boy. When they set me free, that is when my time will come.'

'I have friends on the outside and they have been watching him, I know where he lives, I know where he works, I know he has a wife and children. He didn't plan this through, farmer boy. He thought I was a dull German that he could easily outwit but I have spent the last three years plotting for the day that I see him again. I am not a violent man but I know how to hurt someone and I am going to make him pay in money and in pain for every day I have spent in this stinking place. By the time I am finished with him he will wish he had been sent to prison instead of me, I promise you.'

Torben lent back and looked into the distance. Along the corridors we could hear the jingle jangle of keys and clank of cells doors being locked.

'What about you, how are your plans, farmer boy?'

So far I had not an inkling of what I could do after leaving prison. With all my heart I want to return to Kate and my family and start over again but there was no sign of a thawing of her attitude to me in her letters, which were curt and to the point.

'I think maybe you need to show her that you are able to change,' Torben stated. 'Maybe you should write and ask her what you need to do to prove that you deserve her love rather than just saying what you are doing. A year is not a long time, farmer boy, you will be outside and you must have a plan. You must always have a plan.'

It was time to go back to our cells. I was looking for something to read before the evening finished.

'You should try the Mask book,' said Torben. 'No prisoner wants to read it but it has an interesting story. It is an escape from here at least, you might enjoy it.'

——

'What are you writing, farmer boy?'

Torben's voice drifted through the windowless bars in my cell. It was late evening and I had found that if I could get my mind to calm down, sometimes fully formed ideas would arrive but now I was having some strange and unusual thoughts. Ideas that revolved around the book of the Mask. So I told him that I was playing with some notions and suggestions that have come into my head and I thought that if I were to write them down on my slate they might form something interesting.

'You are taking my advice.'

Yes, Torben, though I wouldn't say I was taking it, more it was something that he had insisted I should do for as long as we had discussed my problems and now it was time to put it into practice. Thoughts used to erupt and rebound around my head and change my whole purpose but now in the confines of my cell I had the time to examine them. Are they reasonable or are they unreasonable, are they achievable in the short term or what circumstances would make them achievable in the future? Or are they pipedreams, without any possibility but for the actions of fate? You cannot plan for fate. You have to make these chances arise and then take them, but why would I, a prisoner in a dank cell in Pentonville have any hope for a turn on the wheel of fortune?

There is the Mask.

Why is the Mask an interesting thought? After all I am not Philipe, the twin brother of the King. If I wear a mask no one will know me. What possible advantage does that give me and who would want to meet such a person?

It hides my identity. I can be someone else. I can be nobody.

Who wants to meet a nobody?

That is a problem. Just because someone is wearing a mask does that make them interesting? In fact they are less interesting, we cannot see their face therefore we don't know them and cannot trust them but they can be mysterious.

Mysterious. Do I mean mystical?

No, I don't mean mystical, that would involve spiritual powers that I do not have and cannot claim. I just mean mysterious in that my identity is blurred and because of my ability to impersonate using my voice I could be someone else. A nobody in a mask, can be somebody.

'You are writing a lot, farmer boy.'

'I am, Torben.'

Because there is a lot to think about. It is not a plan but there is something here in this idea of a mask and I believe I can find the way to make it work for me. My first aim is to win back the love of my wife, maybe not in the short term but in the longer term. All my letters to her saying that I think of her every day, that I wish her well, that I hope the children are healthy and happy, they get no response beyond the bare acknowledgement of their receipt. If I write to Kate and say I want to prove to her that I will stay faithful and provide for her every need as soon as I am released and this plan that I have will ensure our happiness I feel sure that she will listen and at least give me the opportunity to try to win her back.

Torben's voice broke my train of thought. 'And what is your plan?'

'I don't know yet but I have a year to think of it. It will involve a mask, or at least it will be inspired by a mask'.

'Come and see me when you are released, I might be in a position to help you.'

Now that, Torben, is a plan I can follow.

Slate

Pentonville, 1907

From then on every evening I would take to my chalk and slate, thinking of the mask and how it could be my ticket back to my family. The mask itself was not the plan and it took me a while to realise this. The mask would not, could not be anything but a way of hiding the real intention. With all the style of a seasoned magician, the legerdemain would happen elsewhere but what could be the real trick? What sleight of hand could I play?

I knew what I would not do. I would not do anything that would land me in prison again, so it must not be illegal in any way.

I pondered upon the book 'The Man in the Iron Mask'. It is a work of fiction thinly based upon a real event. Why could I not put together a theatre on the street? A few props, an interesting story and I would be an actor in a play. I imagined crowds as I told my ... my what exactly? Why would there be crowds? Why would they give me money? More likely they would pelt me with rotten fruit.

I must not give way to despairing thoughts, that is not the answer but there is something in this concept. A theatre of the street, I shall note that.

On further nights I would explore different avenues.

What about a feat of endurance? The man in the iron mask will ... what could I do? I could sit with my mask on, day in day out in all weathers. Sing songs from the hymnal. No, that would not work. Smash crockery with my head, no that sounds expensive. I do not know the answer but a feat of endurance has a ring to it. I shall note it.

Who is the man in the mask? Of course nobody knows but they will hear my voice, so who shall I resemble? A Norfolk man? Not likely, they would not be impressed by that. I need to use my gentlemanly accent because everyone knows that money comes to money.

Then I would come back to some themes that I liked. A feat of endurance and combined with street theatre. I could be a walking play, promenading around Britain as the man in the iron mask. That does sound good but it seems to lack some magic. There are parts missing, I still cannot understand why I am walking or how, beyond the mere performance I am going to make a profit.

How do people make money? I need to sell them something, something that has a value of its own. Why would they buy something from me? Beyond my appearance and my mystery what do I have to sell?

A souvenir of my feat, an object that would confer some of the glamour of the enterprise to the purchaser. A photograph, or a postcard, a memento that has its own utility.

Why do I walk? What motivates the need for a mask beyond my own need to hide my identity? They won't give me money, why should they? A common criminal, fraudster and bigamist, they will lock me up and throw away the key.

Away with the bad thoughts, there is an answer, I just have to find it within me.

There was another book, 'Around the world in eighty days'. The title tells the story, I have not read it but everyone knows it. There was a bet. Now there is an angle I have not explored. A wager, between the masked walker and ... no one comes to mind. For how much? A lot of money of course. Then why would anyone buy my souvenirs? Because it is part of the wager, the terms are that I must support myself throughout the journey.

That is brilliant, by buying the postcards they are not merely buying a souvenir but investing in the success of the venture.

I have to be careful though. To walk around the world suggests a circumambulation. The main problem is I don't want to set myself a task of physically walking around the world. I need only to travel and spend time in places where I can make money. Britain mainly, then perhaps my fame would have spread abroad and maybe there will be profit in carrying it on and on.

That sounds ambitious?

Yes, but it is the unbridled ambition of the project that will ignite the interest of the public and encourage them to loosen their purses. That is what this whole enterprise needs. An extraordinary wager, a remarkable feat, a spectacle on the street and most importantly the rapturous attention of a crowd.

Kate's kitchen – 2

Thetford, November, 1908

'That's a big story Harry.'

'It is rather long, do you think I should reduce it, Kate?'

'I don't think they need to know all that, just enough so they get the gist of it.'

'I think you are right Kate, let's think what can be done. Hmm, I often brooded upon my fate in prison. Truth be told I was nothing more than a common labourer, with no trade and no experience of business. Competition for work amongst unskilled workmen was hard and so I realised that I must rely upon my own efforts if I was to make a living in the world. My release from prison was coming near when one day I returned to my cell to find that my library books had been changed. An unseen hand had left me this book called the Man in the Iron Mask and I became entranced by it. I read it over and over. I know it is a fiction but has some basis in fact. Taking the chalk and slate that we all had in our cells I started to play with ideas of living with a mask and being anonymous. I worked through many plots but could not at first see how I could profit from such a scheme. Slowly the thought of walking around the world for a bogus wager formed in my mind. In order for this to work I would need to live in the right circles and have *the time to do it but I reasoned that if I was a gentleman of leisure, I could be that person. After all, I had already proved I could imitate the talk of the gentry and having a mask and being anonymous meant I could do it again. I explored the idea further, making up various terms and conditions so that my audience would believe that my walking fiction was a reality. Finally I clearly saw the hundred-thousand dollar wager suggesting that an anonymous American had made the bet. It was audacious, glamorous and daring. I was abuzz with the idea when they released me from prison.'*

'That's good, Harry, I think that captures it. Now tell us what happened next...'

Costume

The walk of a free man, the sound of a door closing that you never want to open again. The smell of my old clothes, musty and dank. Thirty shillings burning a hole in my pocket and a plan for the future.

A brisk walk down the Caledonian Road to King's Cross. From there through the back streets to Long Acre where Stanford's, the cartographers to the King sell maps and stationery with which I could plan out my route. While I was there I made enquiries amongst the staff as to where I might find a theatrical costumier as the Mask was the most important part of my plan. I was told that Clarkson's Wigs of Wardour Street was well known amongst the theatres of London and this was not even ten minutes walk away. I could not miss it they said, it had a large clock above the door.

Indeed as I walked along Wardour Street this new emporium stood out as a beacon because of the ornate clock with 'Costumier' and 'Perruquier' advertising the time and trade all along the road. I felt I knew this place already as it had some fame amongst prisoners at the gaol for offering unusual disguises.

The door, flanked by two shiny brass plaques is opened by a rather outlandish individual with a grand sweep of his arm. Much to my alarm he addresses me in French.

'*Voulez-vous entrer, monsieur?*'

I have no idea what he said but he registered my blank face and adjusted his look so that it felt that he almost saw straight through me. He pursed his lips thoughtfully before saying,

'Come in, come in, don't get cold on the threshold. What little intrigue are you planning and how may I assist you?'

He was quite the most solicitous of individuals and it took all my energy to resist telling him every detail of my venture. Finally I pulled myself together and replied that I was taking a role in a play and needed to have a mask to cover my identity. He put his arm firmly around my shoulders and brought me into close proximity with his bearded face.

'Tell me all, sir, tell me all. We have a mask for every occasion, a Venetian ball, a Greek tragedy, a highway robber if that is your part. Who is this masked man and what play are you undertaking and more importantly when and where will I be able to see you on the stage?'

He had quite the most overwhelming personality that I had ever come across. To be in his company was to feel as though one had drunk long into the night on fine wine. It had been several years since I had sparred in conversation with such a dangerous individual.

'My play is taking form as we speak. The playwright is a new one and he has written a role which requires me for a short while to be unrecognisable.'

'Is it a comedy or is it a drama? When and where is it set? *Pardonnez-moi, s'il vous plait. Madame, vous êtes divine.* You should take that hat, the West End will be at your feet. *Éternelle.* Sorry, where was I?'

'It's in the nature of a drama. In some respects the audience are not entirely sure what they are watching, it's partially a fantasy and therefore allows some leeway to the mask itself.'

'What about a *masque d'épée*, a fencing mask such as this?'

He held up a mask with a mesh front.

'I'll try it but it seems to me to not cover my identity as well as I would hope.'

He shrugged, 'I think that is part of its success, in your role you could suggest that other players cannot recognise you but you and the audience of course would be co-conspirators. What fun you could have with that.'

'Indeed, I see what you are saying but I believe it is the playwright's intent that the audience are left in doubt as to my identity as I am pretending to be one of the other players and am not unmasked until much later in the third act. Do you have anything that meets that particular specification?'

'So you wish to hoodwink the audience. Are you sure it is a play, it is curiously constructed? So something that covers all of your head. Hmm. We have some elaborate cloth head-dresses of middle eastern design, turbans and suchlike. There was a pantomime of Aladdin that recently folded but we had already made some costumes for them. Let's see what we have.'

He walked to the back of the shop and an assistant brought forward two examples.

'This is a plain white keffiyeh. The scarf goes over your head and the band keeps it tight. Now you can bring this part of the scarf over the front of your face and tie it back, to keep it in place. How is that? You look quite the *chevalier Arabe*, if I may say so.'

'It is an interesting idea, how much would you be selling this for?'

'There is a lot of fine workmanship in this costume and I believe this particular article is authentic to the region, so, we may be able to sell it to you for let's say, five guineas.'

'Five guineas, is a little rich for me.'

'Of course we can offer our hire service. If you have a short run, such as a week, that could be the answer. A week would be half a guinea. A month would be a guinea and if you wanted it for a longer period, if you are experiencing a triumph and we all hope for that and a long run throughout the British Isles, then you could purchase it. The hire charge would be taken off the purchase price. I do think that would be your best option.'

'Your terms are very acceptable but I am not sure that the middle eastern motif would be easy to work into our little play. Do you have anything, more British, something historical, maybe?'

He struck his forehead with his clenched hand and looked around his emporium. One wall was filled with wigs of all colours and lengths. On another wall there were hats and scarves. Around the floor there were display cabinets with glass tops showing the various wares beneath. He viewed them all and then turned with a smile.

'I have the very thing' and with that he strode off through a door that lead to a staircase to the basement. He returned a few minutes later, coughing slightly, with what can only be described as a knight's helmet.

'We made the costumes for a Henry IV you know, and one of the suits was damaged by some horseplay. This helmet has no armour, I have not thought of a use for it since we received it back. What do you think? Would it suit your little play, would it allow for your *petit mensonge?*'

I gingerly placed my head inside, it was not easy at first to get the helmet into position but with a tug it came into place. I could feel the weight on my shoulders but I was pleased when I looked into the mirror that I could not easily recognise my face in the visor and although I had a restricted view of the shop, it was ideal.

'I think this will do but what price will it be?'

'This, this trifle we could do for you my little trickster very cheaply. Twenty-five shillings would be sufficient.'

'I like it but I need to talk with my playwright. If I could leave a deposit and pay the balance in a week I think that would be an excellent solution.'

I did not have enough cash to pay for it having already bought the maps and stationery. I could see now that I was going to need a lot more money to start this enterprise.

'Shall we say half a crown? What name shall I put on it?'

And with that I left Mr Clarkson and his emporium of disguise and intrigue.

Foolish

Kate paces around the kitchen of her master's house. She absentmindedly picks up some of the vegetables that had been chosen to accompany the evening meal and sets them down again. Her mind is elsewhere because today is to be a day like no other, a day of reckoning.

She closes her eyes and in her mind she can see the words from Harry's letters. Fine words, filled with beautiful sentiment, about a perfect future where he cares for Kate and their children. Kate is torn though because she knows he can write, he writes like an angel, about what he is going to do and who he will become. Kate has heard it all before, these promises, so easily made. She has no use for promises, she wants a steadfast heart, a loving companion to attend the church and an upstanding man about the town. Despite all her hopes, Kate knows that this cannot happen here in Thetford because although the local people respect her, they will not give Harry such latitude.

Rat-a-tat-tat. The knocker rattles the front door and Kate rushes to open it, catching a black glance from Mrs. Minns the doctor's wife, as she passes the drawing room. Kate is flustered but she supposes he has forgotten the instruction in her last letter to present himself at the back door. Opening it, Kate can barely recognise the man in front of her. A paper thin version of the man she last saw cowed in the dock of the Old Bailey, now with a face full of beard just like pictures of the King. Kate takes his hand and ushers him around to the kitchen door.

'You've come back,' she says once inside the kitchen. 'So what words have you for me?'

Harry looks around the unfamiliar kitchen then stares down at his hands. Slowly he begins to mumble.

'It's my fault Kate, all of it, the last six years have been a terrible mistake and I take the blame for all of it. I never listened to you, even though you always gave me the very best advice but I thought I knew better. I now know I was completely wrong. These years have given me the opportunity to examine and improve myself. If I may be so bold to say that my problem was that I failed to keep a hold of myself and became open to mischief. Prison has taught me well, it has straightened me out. I am truly sorry for every calamity that I caused and I am ready to begin again for your sake and for Lily and Alice.'

Kate stood impassive, listening to his unfamiliar accent. Finally she replied.

'You are right though, it's not just me Harry, it's Alice and Lily. You can't just walk in here and expect us to start all over. Things are broken deep between us and just because you are here now does not mean that it's all mended. If you want to be a family, you have to prove that we can trust you and that you deserve our trust. That won't happen overnight. You can't just turn up and expect the last six years to be forgot. '

'But we have to put this behind us Kate. I have done bad things and I have paid a terrible price. I have borne the punishment that the law required and now I am willing to make the sacrifice to win the hearts of my family.'

'Pretty words' Kate says with an icy tone. 'Pretty words, Harry, you know what them suffragettes say is right. It's deeds not words that count. That's what I want from you. Live a good life, a Godly life, it's what you do that is the mark of you, because I've heard all the things you say and they never hold true.'

'I have me a plan, Kate, I have a plan to make us all rich and happy.'

'Them's just more fine words Harry,' says Kate with a steely look. 'You come back and see me when you've made your fortune and we'll see where we go from there. Until then you'd better go find your sister and see if her family will put you up because there's no place for you here.'

—

Harry stands proud in his Sunday suit and smiles as Kate shepherds Alice and Lily into the church. Kate acknowledges Harry and takes her place in the pew next to him but they do not speak. Once the service starts Harry sings out, his clear voice undoubtedly the finest in the parish. Alice and Lily shyly take short surreptitious glances at this stranger from behind their mother's dress. At the end of the service Harry kneels down and hugs his children with an emotional embrace and they melt into his arms.

'I suppose you've heard my news?' He says afterwards in the churchyard. Kate has heard whispers but she can barely believe it.

'I've got a job' he says.

'What kind of job is this Harry? A walking job, pushing a perambulator about, that's no employment I've heard of, not unless you're taking a baby for a stroll and I know you're not doing that.'

That's not all Kate has heard, people have told her that he's bought this perambulator and had it painted with strange signs. Then he's been seen at the railway station getting off the London train several times and there has been rumours of him having his picture taken and photographs made, not to mention buying clothes and getting pamphlets printed by the town's printer. All these things cost money and Harry has no job and no income and there is not a chance that any of these people would extend Harry credit, not with his record.

'It's just a wager,' he says. 'When I win, we'll be rich but in the meantime while I sell my trinkets we'll have a tidy little wage, you wait and see. I'll send you money every week and keep you up to date with where I am and then when all is ready you can join me on the road. I'll have a caravan and a horse for you and the girls. We'll find teachers on the route and all I ask is that you'll come to me when I call.'

Kate makes no reply but inside she is seething. She cannot understand how Harry can think that he has a plan at all, to her it is just a dream. What is more she knows that Harry has criss-crossed the town telling all and sundry his business, including that he's supposed to keep himself a secret until it's all over! This is one huge flaw that takes her breath away because she knows that

Thetford is full of blabbermouths and a secret should be a secret, not something the whole town shares. For Kate the most damning part of the whole escapade is that she wonders who these people are with wealth so enormous they could stake such a wager and why would they choose Harry as their hireling? That is a huge unanswered question as Harry is not for telling.

To walk round the world? That won't take a week, it won't take a year, it could take a lifetime. He could walk off into the distance and Kate would never see him again. It is bad enough that Harry will leave but Kate cannot believe it is for such a foolish, foolish plan and wants nothing to do with it.

Kate's kitchen – 3

Thetford, November, 1908

'Harry let's stop here and think about what we've got.'

'It's very tricky Kate. I need to tell you the truth but I'm not sure I want to tell the world exactly what happened.'

'No, we need to shorten this part to just the events and nothing more.'

'All right, let's start from here. They gave me thirty shillings when I left prison and I immediately went into central London and bought an atlas of the British Isles and some pens and paper. Then I went to Clarkson's, the theatrical costumiers and inspected several masks before putting a deposit down on one of them. Finally that day I went home and saw my wife and children. As the days went by I told the townspeople of my new employment by a gentleman and the plan to walk round the world and to my surprise and delight they were all eager to help. One of my neighbours offered an old perambulator which I could use and pay for later but I knew I needed more money to start the enterprise. I travelled back up to London and met up with an old

acquaintance from prison, a German fellow of superior education and some social standing. I let him into my confidence about the whole scheme and he offered to finance me, adding that he could help in other ways as well. Of course, this offer of help was welcome and if I was to put the plan in motion I had to accept, though he extracted a heavy price for his assistance. Leaving this meeting I returned to Clarkson's and bought the mask. Even with the extra money there were still further expenses. I got a handy five pounds by way of security from a young man I engaged to accompany me on my walk. In lieu of wages, I would pay his board and lodging along the way and I proposed to give him a third of the wager on the successful completion of the walk, though he would forfeit the money if he left beforehand. I had the perambulator painted and inscribed and finally had pamphlets and postcards printed. We were ready to start the walk but first one of the conditions I omitted to mention was that I should find a wife on the road. I already had a wife and I intended that she should join us as soon as I could afford suitable conveyance for her use.'

'Do you think you should put that in Harry? It never happened'

'I think you will find it will be helpful.'

Off

New Year's Day, 1908

She won't see me. I can't believe she won't bring the children to see me off. It's so unfair to let me go without at least saying goodbye but she will not budge. This is a desperate day and no mistake. All I want is the approval of my wife and it would all be fine. She refuses to see that she can join us once the show is rolling, the plan allows for it, with the finding a wife clause.

She did not see it that way, though.

'Why do you have to find a wife? You've already got one.'

'I need to make the people think that I found my wife on the way because if I had been married before, suspicious people might do checks and discover who I really am but if I found you on the way Kate, then obviously we are not previously related so your name and circumstances have no bearing on the man in the mask. I don't want to be unmasked. It is the very mysteriousness of my identity that makes this work. No one is going to give a gaolbird a penny to walk round the world but a gentleman on a challenge is a very different proposition.'

There's a knock. That'll be Albert, on time, good man. He's a stickler. Poor sap, he thinks he's off to make his fortune. It's a shame really but when you need some cash you've got to use what you can and his five pounds was very welcome. I'll look after him though, he will be well fed and watered once we're underway. I let him in and we go through the equipment in the perambulator one last time before we walk to the station.

'Are you ready to put the mask on?' he says.

I suppose I am but the thought is unsettling. It is everything I have planned for and yet this could all just go wrong in an instant. I must be bold but I feel the nerves jangling all around my body. I hold the shiny helmet up above my head and tip it forward slowly before easing the iron collar over my face. Darkness descends. The slits of the visor edge into view and the light of the room shafts into my face. The collar rests on my shoulders and for the first time I fully appreciate the weight of the helmet.

Albert puts on his flat cap and coat while I take a firm hold of the perambulator.

'You're off then.' It's my younger sister Alice, standing with her arms folded in the doorway of the little kitchen looking sceptically at me.

'It's time to go, Alice, it's time for me to take my travelling show on the road and present myself to the British public. Thank you for all your hospitality, here is five pounds to help pay for my lodging and goodbye until we meet again.'

The air nips at us as we leave the house and tramp to the station. The barely lit streets are empty of people and if we are to make our rendezvous at Trafalgar Square we need to leave early in order to catch the train to Cambridge and change there for the London line. The station itself is almost the only well-lit place in Thetford and in the pools of electric light a few passengers are rubbing their hands and stamping their feet as they wait to catch the early train. So far no one has taken any notice of me whatsoever which causes me both relief and consternation. Relief because, despite everything I am not sure I am ready yet for what is about to happen. Consternation because what if this is the reaction and nothing happens? What if nobody cares? Worse still, what if they just all laugh at me? Am I wasting my time? All that hard work and planning, let alone the expense, will it all end before it has even begun?

We enter the station and I can hear the distant call of the train as it approaches the outskirts of Thetford. I present my ticket to the station inspector, who makes no comment about my strange attire as he ushers me through. Albert follows but he is stopped when the inspector sees the perambulator.

'Have you got a ticket for that?'

I am walking across to the Cambridge platform and I realise that Albert has been held back. People are looking up and around because of the argument between the Inspector and Albert. I am frozen by indecision. I should go back and help and yet at the same time I don't want to be stared at, mocked and ridiculed before I have even started.

'I did not know we needed a ticket for the perambulator.' Somehow I had turned and was addressing the inspector using my best upper class accent. He looks directly at me for the first time, then he regards the perambulator and its signage. I could feel the eyes of all the passengers on that station platform were upon us.

'Remarkable – and what are these?' He holds up some of the merchandise stored in the perambulator.

'Postcards and pamphlets, souvenirs of our journey. Here, take one and thank you for assisting us.'

'What an amazing feat, to walk round the world.'

'It starts today.'

'Then I must be the first to support you, sir,' and to my surprise he put his hand in his pocket and handed over a silver sixpence and with that the most incredible scene unfolded. All of the passengers crowded around the perambulator asking for postcards, photographs and pamphlets. I was so overwhelmed by the stir of the crowd that at first I was awkward and shy but the realisation that this was exactly the reaction I had planned for all those years in prison gave me inner strength. Within minutes we had sold souvenirs to all the waiting people. We were off and in business before we had even set foot on the train.

We journeyed to Cambridge and then on to London managing to get a compartment to ourselves, which prevented interruption and long discussion with the other passengers. The breaking dawn failed to brighten the sky but brought more gloom as the day was misty. On arrival in London we hired a hansom cab and journeyed through the strangely worsening fog to Charing Cross Station where I had a rendezvous with an old friend before the big event.

He was waiting at the forecourt, head and shoulders above the rest of the populace wearing a smart black coat and crisp bowler hat looking very much the English gentleman. Albert helped me to unload the perambulator as my friend watched with interest.

'So this is my investment. It certainly makes an impression, well done my friend, I think we will make a big success of today. I have alerted the press and I believe there is a reporter and photographer from one of the national papers waiting in the square. Here is your pedlar's license, that is the last expense. So, does that visor lift? Then face the wall and take a sip from my hip flask, you will need some schnapps to get the blood moving on this cold morning. Come now, we shall go and find the reporters in time to begin this enterprise. What time did you plan to start?'

'Ten thirty is the plan.'

'We've just missed the chimes of ten o'clock. Let's hurry to the Square, that should give the reporters enough time for a brief interview and a photograph. It's all looking good, I like the look of the postcards and the fact that you have a large number as well, I see. More than your allotted one pound's worth I would wager, still who's counting but I hope you sell them.'

'I'll need to sell them and many more to pay you back Torben, but we have sold some already this morning. We were mobbed at the station.'

'That is a good omen. Show me the takings.'

Albert opened his case to show the cash. Torben leaned in close and whispered, 'Don't forget farmer boy, one-third of all that you take is mine.'

A gentle hubbub reverberated around Trafalgar Square as we crossed the road to the centre as couples and families were taking in the New Year air. Torben introduced us to a reporter from the Daily Mirror who asked about the wager.

Torben looked at his watch, and with just a few moments to go I steadied myself to deliver, in my best upper class accent, a small speech I had prepared to the growing crowd of people.

'Today I begin a magnificent task. To walk around the world while wearing an iron mask. This wager came about as the result of an argument that took place at a gentleman's club. An American millionaire declared that no Englishman would walk round the world, masked and pushing a perambulator. On hearing these conditions I at once made up my mind to accept. Starting from here in London I intend to traverse the entire British Isles and then cross five continents. I will visit all the major cities of the greatest countries in the world and upon my return reveal my identity and God willing thereby win this, the largest wager on record. During this challenge I cannot expend any more of my own money than this one pound note I hold here. I must support myself and my assistant entirely from the sale of these postcards, photographs and pamphlets. I can receive no charity, not even a sip of water without payment being made. Because of this, I look to you the great British public to support and encourage me. There are the chimes of Big Ben at ten thirty so it is time for me to say goodbye to you all and look forward to the day when I hear those chimes again. I will see you in ten years.'

With that I firmly gripped the handle of the perambulator and began to walk towards the Strand. The pace was hindered by the press of the crowd. Albert was selling postcards, photographs and pamphlets as quick as he was able and I was fielding questions with as much charm as I could muster but progress was slow.

The cheering and shouting seemed to just bring more people close to see what was going on and soon we were barely moving at all. The helmet muffled the sound of the crowd but somehow brought them very close, too close for comfort and through it all I heard the chimes of eleven o'clock and we had barely reached the start of the Strand. Did it matter? No, not one bit, because I could see that Albert's leather caddy was weighing heavily on his shoulder as it filled with coin, the postcards selling as fast as we could hand them out. I turned around and caught sight of Torben following our progress from a distance, a huge smile evidencing his delight with the successful launch of the venture.

We progressed along the Strand, the pace slowly picking up after the crawl out of the Square. Some people are following us, others becoming aware of the commotion join the throng. I was glad that I had paid out for the sign writing on the perambulator because it told the main story but the questions came thick and fast nonetheless. I answer as best I can.

'Where are you going?'

'Across the face of the Earth and if you buy this pamphlet at a very reasonable price you will see the full itinerary'.

'How long will it take?'

'Ten years, I expect.'

'Who made the wager?'

'I cannot reveal their identities but there is an American millionaire and a British Lord involved.'

'Why you?'

'I am an Englishman of their acquaintance and that is how it came about.'

'Who are you?'

'The rules of the challenge mean that I cannot reveal my identity until the task is complete. The pamphlet sets out all the conditions and is priced at a very reasonable sixpence. Perhaps a photograph for a shilling, so that your friends or loved ones can know that you were here on this historic day?'

Questions, the same questions with little variation. Around us the crowd jostles, only the faces change in the surrounding scrum. People are captured by the romance of the challenge and for a time escort us along the streets, perhaps believing that they too are about to walk out of their lives and around the world. If they did believe it, that was more than I did.

There are others who are more scornful and to those sceptical voices I can hear in my head different answers to their questions.

'Where am I going?'

'I'll disappear as quick as the crowds.'

'How long will it take?'

'Not long and I'll be gone but I'll take your coin before I go.'

'Who made the wager?'

'I'm not cheating you, you are buying a souvenir of my travelling theatre, enjoy the atmosphere, promenade with the show, it will make you feel ten feet tall.'

'Why you?'

'You are addressing the producer and artiste all in one, I conjured this spectacle to enchant you. Don't waste your breath questioning it.'

'Who are you?'

'I know who I am, I am the man with the imagination to make this happen and you sir or madam, you are my audience.'

The walking is slow but we are making progress, we need to pick up the pace if only to allow fresh people to see us and buy our wares. We walk along Fleet Street, passing the main offices of the London newspapers, all of which were open as they write the stories for the next day. Here we are bringing the news to the papers, another of Torben's excellent ideas.

From Fleet Street we walk on to St Paul's Cathedral where there is a press of people. We are grabbing money almost from the air and by this time my throat is dry and I am hungry but it is unrelenting as we continue on down Cheapside to London Bridge.

The Thames crossing is cold, the fog has lifted but the wind is beginning to roar. South of the River many of our impromptu entourage are fatigued or bored and slowly fade away but still more people come to see the spectacle and buy our wares as we make our way down the Old Kent Road.

Dusk is coming. The day never brightened and the gloom is drawing closer. The streets begin to empty and we need to find a bed for the night. We take rooms at the Guy, Earl of Warwick tavern in Welling. Exhausted from the walking and the constant attentions of the public we rest on our beds.

There is a knock on the door. Then a quiet whisper. 'It's me'

Torben has arrived to see how well his investment is doing. 'Let us see the takings.'

Albert and I empty our leather caddies onto the bed. There is a mountain of silver coins. We start to make them into piles of pounds.

'How many postcards did you have?'

'I had a thousand made, I think they are nearly sold. The photographs and pamphlets are not so popular but if we sell out of the postcards then they will help.'

The piles of coin get larger and larger. Finally the count is over. Torben checks and then double checks his figures.

'Seventeen pounds, four shillings and eleven pence. That is an excellent first day. My cut will be five pounds and ten shillings and I will pay for supper tonight. We will take it in the room and then later, once you are refreshed you can maybe visit the tavern and sell some more goods. Meanwhile tomorrow I will find a photographer and a printer so that you can replenish your stocks.'

'Can't I just go downstairs and take supper in the tavern. They don't know my face.'

'Certainly not my friend, there are more ways of recognising a person than just their face. To go about without being recognised you would need to change your attire and your physique. I cannot have you being unmasked on the first night, or on any other night for that matter. All meals, all refreshments need to be taken in strict privacy and that includes away from the serving staff.'

'Albert, find a waitress and we will order supper.'

On Friday morning we had barely left the tavern and started to make our way along the Broadway only to be stopped by an overzealous officer of the law. He asked me if I had a pedlar's certificate and I referred him to Albert. The truth was that Torben had arranged for Albert to have the certificate and not me mainly because the certificate had the inconvenience of requiring me to reveal my identity. So I obviously made the constable aware of this and tried to make light of the situation by saying, 'I don't go from house to house selling.' However the constable who was probably still nursing a hangover from the New Year celebrations was in no mood for idle chit-chat and took us both directly to the police station. This was a calamitous turn of events. Barely two days into the walk and it was all going to end.

Torben was still keeping close attendance and he stepped in to find a local solicitor, a Mr. Clinch, a small elderly gentleman with a quick intelligence and a keen eye for detail who came up with an ingenious plan to avoid being unmasked. Firstly, once Torben made it known that he would be amply rewarded for his services, Clinch worked hard to ensure that the case was dealt with the next day, a Saturday, otherwise we could have been delayed in Bexleyheath for up to a week. Next he suggested that I should use a 'nom de plume' because without one they would be unlikely to let me even have bail. Henry Mason was the name we agreed upon. Thirdly, with Torben he spoke to the press, because he was strongly of the opinion that this was a case where the public would have a great interest and in this he was proven correct.

At Dartford police court the next day there was a large crowd outside cheering as we made our way in. Inside the courtroom the press box was filled with local and national reporters eager to see the outcome of the case.

Mr. Clinch was a sharply intelligent man who relished his moment in the limelight. The magistrates were at first inclined to be stringent on the letter of the law but Mr. Clinch was able to make them see that this was not the start of a sinister crime wave in Bexleyheath. He questioned whether the public interest would be served by bringing this harmless enterprise to halt, the public so far being keen supporters as witnessed by the crowds both in and out of the courtroom. He went on to say that this remarkable challenge would be ended there and then, should I be required to remove my headgear and give my real name.

Mr Clinch's words worked as if they were balm on the magistrates, who let me keep my helmet on and more importantly, realising that the enterprise relied on my anonymity, allowed me to continue using my alias. The mood lightened once these items had been dealt with and I was greatly relieved. The case then turned into a light comic operetta as the magistrates considered the other conditions of the wager. The finding a wife condition had them particularly exercised, with even the prosecution joining in and suggesting that wearing a mask would be a deep encumbrance to such an endeavour. There was general laughter when it was suggested I would have better luck in another less fortunate part of the borough, where I might not only find a wife but could then use the perambulator as a convenient way to carry her about.

Finally the chairman of the magistrates was inclined to bring the proceedings to an end. He felt this was not a serious crime and under normal circumstances a pedlar would be locked up for the night and set free the next day. Noting that we had been bailed and therefore avoided detention he fined us half a crown, warned us to have the proper license in future and to keep out of the courts because they would likely not be so lenient on a second occasion. To my great relief we were free to continue.

There was delirious cheering in the court room and an even more rapturous reception from the crowds outside as we left the building. Mr. Clinch was paid handsomely for his services and he probably dined out on the story for many years.

We had however lost out on two days of earnings but the publicity that came from the court case more than made up for it. In the street outside the courthouse every postcard and pamphlet that we had was snatched out of our hands. Torben had to make arrangements with the photographers to have thousands of copies printed for us and rushed to our hotel as the demand far exceeded supply. From now on we were careful to ensure that any cash was given only to Albert who would place it diligently in his satchel. We also vowed to keep our eyes peeled to ensure that we avoided the attentions of the police.

The money we were taking was becoming a serious encumbrance and it became necessary to open a bank account so we could continue our journey without risking the interest of robbers and bandits. Seeing this problem, Mr Clinch took us to a nearby bank where he was well known to the manager. It was necessary again to use an alias and Henry Mason became the third invisible party to our enterprise. From then on making a deposit for Henry as we called it, was a common occurrence.

Torben was more problematic. He had paid the court costs and decided that as the level of his investment in the venture had increased significantly, his rewards should see a commensurate increase. He now wanted half of our takings and what's more he wanted to become a signatory to the bank account so that he could collect his income at any time without the inconvenience of following our travels around the country. I protested that I would pay him back for the court costs and I was desperate to keep the original arrangement but Torben would have none of it. He said that without his help we would not have had such a wily campaigner as Mr Clinch on our side and the whole enterprise would have ended calamitously. He was asking for more money due to the risky nature of his investment and also as a reward for the time and effort he had made on my behalf. Regretfully, I acceded to his wishes.

I sent a letter to Kate, telling her not to worry because we had won the court case and now we were free to carry on. I enclosed a postal order for ten pounds for her and the children and I beseeched Kate to contact me through Torben, as he would often meet with us and be able to deliver letters to me.

Back on the road, despite the cold and misty weather, the crowds are if anything even larger than before and what's more they seem to know who I am and what I am doing. I am celebrated and revered, famous throughout the land. People shout and cheer when I come close. Mayors and dignitaries await my arrival and make great speeches.

At the same time I can feel the helmet on my shoulders, the perambulator vibrating my whole body, my arms ache, my hands are numb and my legs and feet are heavy with tiredness. From inside the visor, the world seems distant and insignificant and there are long periods as we leave the metropolis where it is just Albert and me tramping the dusty roads. Carriages pass, occasionally a smelly motor car will fill my ears with noise, my eyes with dust and the helmet with noxious fumes. How anyone can find joy in that activity I do not know.

Days go by and slowly the terrible tiredness that overcomes my body every evening begins to drain away. I no longer need to immediately take a bath and then rest on my bed when we arrive at a town and find our lodging for the evening. Albert has bought me an alternative outfit with a hat and scarf as evening-wear. Then there are furtive occasions despite the warnings from Torben when I leave our lodging and find a public house out of the way of our route to enjoy an evening of food and drink. Talking to the local people I use a regular London accent, which causes some interest but as it is not the same as the masked man, who is known to be a gentleman, I am in no danger of being recognised. Quite often in conversation the subject of the Iron Mask comes up, especially as it is the news of the day. I find myself musing along as to his identity and we have long discussions about what we would do with the money, if any of us were lucky enough to win it. A thought that often goes through my mind, wishing that the wager was real.

Poor Albert meanwhile has to make his own arrangements as if we were seen together I am sure I would be unmasked. He tells me he does not enjoy going out as he is easily recognised and finds himself continually pestered for information about the whole enterprise and me in particular. Consequently Albert, generally a genial soul who loves company, now prefers to stay in his room away from the public.

Despite Torben being able to access the bank account he often visits us along the way. He counts the money and audits the stock and is quick to express his disappointment when the takings are down. I explain that we are no longer walking through streets with houses lined with people, now there are long stretches of countryside, which is only to be expected and the towns when we do arrive are much smaller than the vast sprawl of London. Still Torben is unsatisfied and believes that we are not making enough of our opportunity. About a week into the walk, he comes up with a plan that when we reach the next large town we should stay there for two or three days and promenade as much as possible so as to maximise our earnings. He would also make sure that we got a grand a civic reception by alerting the mayor and the local newspaper ahead of our arrival.

The most precious thing that Torben did was give me a letter from Kate. I waited for him to leave and once alone, I read it.

Dear Harry,

Thank you for your letter and the Postal Order.

I have bought new Sunday dresses for Alice and Lily and an outfit for myself. The rest of the money we are going to use to have a little holiday in Cromer later in the year. Although I am grateful for your money I wish that you had not left us. I have seen the newspapers and articles about you. I was shocked to read of your arrest but glad that they set you free. I still don't believe this tale of you walking around the world.

I want you to give up this foolishness and come home to be a proper father again.

Yours Truly

Kate

Artiste

The perambulator is a heavy beast with spindly wheels that feel every rut and bump. It lacks even the most rudimentary suspension so the undulations of the road transmit directly to my hands and arms. Each day before heading off, Albert and I clean the paintwork and oil the wheels but despite this necessary care I can see that the wood of the carriage is starting to dry out and crack. The metal wheels which I once thought light and airy and gave the perambulator a refined look, are in reality thin and delicate. Fine for walking about a town but not up to the task of rutted country roads.

Maidstone is our next stop and it is obvious that Torben has been hard at work. On the outskirts despite the wet and cold there is a gaggle of boys and girls who shout and cheer us on our way into the centre. A constable stops us and tells us he will lead us to the welcoming party. We walk through the streets with crowds gathering along the pavement, a raggedy procession with the constable in front, us in the centre and a long tail of hangers-on and dogs. All the while we are selling merchandise as fast as we can. At the front of the Town Hall a large crowd has gathered and the mayor greets us while a band plays nearby, people are laughing and cheering and the whole town feels as though it is swollen with pride at our presence. The large figure of Torben weaves his way through the wash of people and tells me to announce that I will be making a special appearance at the Hippodrome tomorrow night. I am invited by the dignitaries to make a short speech.

'Thank you, thank you, Lord Mayor, ladies and gentlemen, boys and girls. We are overwhelmed by the warmth of your Maidstone welcome. Thank you most sincerely. I am the Man in the Iron Mask and I am on an epic journey to walk round the world. It will not be easy, there will be many hardships to endure but when we receive generous hospitality such as we are witnessing here today, it gives us new strength. It is only due to your support and encouragement that we can hope to complete this venture. Our success therefore is also your success. To remember this day and show your dedication to our cause please help us by purchasing our merchandise. Tomorrow evening I will be making an appearance on the stage of the Hippodrome and we will be resting here in Maidstone for a few days.'

The crowd cheered and clapped and many stayed with us for another two hours while we sold our wares in the damp town square. Torben found a local photographer who could take our picture in his studio early next morning and thereby replenish our stocks of postcards. Torben also brought more pamphlets from our printers and the first handful of a steady stream of extraordinary letters from women with proposals of marriage.

The next evening after a fruitful day promenading across the town, I found myself standing on a theatre stage in front of hundreds of people rousing them to help with my cause. An event that happened again and again on my travels because as we quickly realised it was always a lucrative evening.

That night I wrote a letter to Kate and enclosed two ten pound notes. I implored her to come and join me on the road. Never mind that the children will miss their schooling, it can all be sorted out with the money that is coming in.

Inside the mask I live a closed-in life. I walk, of course, I push the perambulator and it turns my hands to jelly with the constant jarring. My legs are strong and my thighs are growing to the size of the trunk of a strong oak tree. However, my feet complain bitterly about the boots and I am a martyr to corns and calluses. Otherwise I am as fit as a fiddle and I find myself acquiring new depths of stamina each day. Our progress so far has been slow especially after losing two days walking because of the court case, so I have upped the pace. This challenge, if I were to undertake the complete walk would be a matter of over thirty-five thousand miles. If I am to do it in ten years I would need to average ten miles a day and so far we have only managed half that speed. I don't know why I am thinking this way, it is almost as if I believe the challenge is real but I feel I must show greater resolve. The more I believe in it the more others will as well, so I need to be aware of my goals and my achievements.

I am telling the reporters that I am writing a journal. I tell them I bought it before I started the walk and in it I am sketching my recollections of places, people and events. It is true that when I meet famous personages I ask them to sign my book and make a suitable comment. I sometimes hope that in the future I may find a way to publish it. Or use it as a basis for a memoir. I am not sure about the detail, maybe I will complete the challenge, I certainly feel that I have the stamina and it is true that the public support makes the walking easier. Maybe I could find a way that the wager will become null and void. Maybe some event will get in my way or maybe I can just auction the book.

Maybe I can be somebody else for the rest of my life. Now there is a thought that won't leave me alone. It would be perfect because here in my mask I lose my past. Before in my previous life I resembled a caterpillar, a lowly grub struggling in the dirt. Now inside my mask I am a chrysalis full of potential to emerge as ... as what exactly? Because the second I take my mask off I will be recognised and I will revert back to being a grub. How do I become that beautiful butterfly?

Kate just wants me to be a grub again. To take the slights and brickbats of our acquaintances and neighbours who look down on us. Who look down on me especially and rightly so, because my foolish past will never be forgotten. So I should labour on a farm for cash or look after the poor souls in the asylum because Kate thinks that is all I deserve.

Look at me now Kate, people rush to see me, they push and shove to buy my wares. They shout and cheer when I go by. They give me a month's pay every day. That is what I deserve. I paid my penance to society in the toil and sweat of Pentonville.

Living on the road is not cheap. There is Torben's tax of course, every pound earned is a pound shared and he has an eagle eye. He knows exactly how much stock we have and therefore how much money we have taken and he's not slow to demand his cut. I wish I did not begrudge him his share as without his contribution all this would be a pipe dream but I do because he has had his investment back, with interest and now he has an enviable income that allows him a lavish lifestyle while I tramp on in the cold and rain.

Then there is the board and lodging. I have to keep young Albert happy as I would be lost without him. His faux American accent is completely forgotten but his appetite has doubled, as has mine. Also I give him a generous salary so he can send money home to his wife and children who he is missing badly.

We are using up boot leather at a fantastic rate and I visit a cobbler in practically every town we pass through. I always complain about the punishment that my feet are taking and one kindly fellow suggested I should try a sandal.

'If it was good enough for the Romans,' he said.

Do you know those ancients were onto something. My feet are in clover despite the rain and wind. I am thinking of throwing away my clod-hopping boots but then I see some huge puddle on the road and put them back on again, even though they are hateful objects and I despise them.

Today is Valentine's Day. We are leaving Brighton after a very profitable three days and Torben has brought yet more marriage proposals. In amongst the letters Kate has written back thanking me for the money but still imploring me to stop. I am thoroughly sick of her bleating, what more can I do? I am making a small fortune and offering her the opportunity of a lifetime to share it with me and she refuses to come.

As we walked through Shoreham a bold lady stopped me and gave me a Valentine's card. Mabel, as she announced herself was very forward, questioning me about the 'find a wife clause' and asking with a glint in her eye if the position was still vacant. I warmed to Mabel as she walked alongside us for over an hour. We chatted with ease while we wound our way to Worthing. I was surprised when Mabel then baldly asked if I would dine with her that evening. Reluctantly I declined as I already had an engagement at the Winter Hall where I was to speak in a break between the showing of films. As we parted, she said that she felt sure that we would meet again.

But I am beginning to wonder Kate, if you are not willing to join me, whether it is time for me to look for a new wife, someone spirited and there is no one more spirited than Mabel.

Tragically in taking my perambulator on to the stage at the Winter Hall, I felt a part of the undercarriage loosen. The next day we patched it up as good as we could and after the daily cleaning and oiling, we pushed on even though the gusting wind and squally rains made our progress difficult. On my instruction Albert purchased a tarpaulin so that we could keep the merchandise and clothing dry in the face of the worsening rain. We found a cord to keep it secure over the top of the perambulator but the wind would catch it and blow rain into the cradle. Despite the weather we walked on as this was a day to show resolve. Of course we lost custom, of course Torben would be displeased, wasting our time walking when we could find a theatre to shelter in and make profit.

Encore

I have found comfort for my feet as I am wearing sandals more and more even when the weather is inclement. It is pure bliss to take a step without the nagging agonies of my corns, so now it is time to turn my attention to the carriage.

The perambulator rattles and vibrates excessively and I am beginning to believe that there is a more significant defect within its body. I will admit I was happy with its look when I first purchased it and once the sign writer had finished his labours the shiny carriage on its own would turn heads with the glossy paintwork and classic lines. I never gave it a good run out before I purchased it to see how it would be on the road. It seems to me that the main problem is the spindly wheels, they transmit and amplify every bump and jolt, causing my fingers to tingle and my arms to ache. I need some cushioning between myself and the road. The bicycles that constantly pass with their large pneumatic tyres are better designed to take the strain. I will need to have a new perambulator as this one is falling apart and Torben will have to pay for his share of it or we will have words.

My sandals squelch through the mud and rain but we keep our spirits up with a song. At the Hippodrome in Brighton I had heard a jolly tune that had the theatre in uproarious laughter so much so that the entertainer came back and made three encores. I took up the song with as much brim and gusto as I could muster.

> When I was in the army
> I was a cavalryman you know
> And whenever I went on parade,
> A magnificent picture I made

For it matters not where I go, It's...

Albert, despite being a shy young man in many ways and especially singing, soon joined in on the chorus.

> *...Bumpety, bumpety, bumpety, bump*
>
> *as if I was riding my charger*
>
> *Bumpety, bumpety, bumpety, bump*
>
> *as proud as an Indian Rajah*
>
> *All the girls declare that I'm a gay old stager*
>
> *Hey, hey, clear the way here comes the galloping major.*

The audience in Brighton had quickly risen to their feet bouncing along to the tune, which I fancied was a regular feature of the bill and we too made the actions of riding the horse and became consumed with laughter. The weather and lack of business were forgotten. I picked up the second verse and Albert hummed along.

> *Last year I thought I'd treat myself*
>
> *To a holiday by the sea*
>
> *So I went and my quarters I fixed*
>
> *Then I found that the bathing was mixed*
>
> *How they giggled as soon as they saw, me...*

Off we went again with the merry dance, those who could see us on the road stopped in the tracks to watch our display.

> *...Bumpety, bumpety, bumpety, bump*
>
> *as if I was riding my charger*
>
> *Bumpety, bumpety, bumpety, bump*
>
> *as proud as an Indian Rajah*
>
> *All the girls declare that I'm a gay old stager*
>
> *Hey, hey, clear the way here comes the galloping major.*

It felt as if we were walking through a shallow sea in this rain as we bumped and splashed our way through the chorus. Albert was dancing around the perambulator kicking up as much water as he could from the puddles and I was pretending to be a prancing horse in front of a carriage. I fancied I remembered the final verse and picked up the song once more.

> *I always was a ladies man*

And a favourite with the sex
Well, I called upon one yesterday
Though I won't give the lady away
For as soon as we sat down to dine, I went...

As we began the chorus another voice joined us.

...Bumpety, bumpety, bumpety, bump
as if I was riding my charger
Bumpety, bumpety, bumpety, bump
as proud as an Indian Rajah
All the girls declare that I'm a gay old stager
Hey, hey, clear the way here comes the galloping major.

The song had ended and I turned and there dancing in the rain was Mabel giggling in a most delightful manner. Mabel joined our merry band and despite the terrible weather we made good speed to Portsea arriving at Totterdell's Hotel with plenty of time for a hot bath and then a late lunch.

Mabel was flirtatiously determined to join in. Fortunately I had a black silken mask which I had made after the events of Bexleyheath and I used this to cover my face when dining because I would never know, even when locked in my own room when the door might be opened. Mabel was first-rate company and as the weather was showing no sign of changing, we opened a bottle of champagne to celebrate our arrival in the warmth and shelter of the hotel.

The wine was excellent and restored full feeling to the body and made me loosen up towards my guest, Mabel Reed from Sussex. A vivacious lady who stated that she was so taken by her meeting with me on Valentine's Day that she saw this as a sign to leave her home and follow me around until I gave in and married her. I have never experienced such a direct approach. The letters I had received with offers of marriage I could scarcely take seriously. Some of them purportedly coming from titled ladies, I read them with amusement but not with any desire for further correspondence. Mabel was flesh and blood and what's more full of the right spirit. I found that my head was being turned by this remarkable lady.

Torben was nearby to oversee events but he could not have foreseen this. He was somewhat taken aback when he entered the dining room of the hotel to find the three of us in happy concert at a lone table singing 'the Galloping Major' one more time. He was not sure what to say but before he said anything I introduced Mabel as my delightful travelling companion and Torben as the tour manager, and then pressed my case for a new perambulator, stating that it was barely possible that I could walk another mile with the old one. Both Mabel and Torben eyed each other with a certain suspicious reserve. The wine had done for me and I could not care what they thought of each other. I made my excuses and retired to my room.

Torben knocked on the door. I understand Torben now, he needs to have things in proper order and this turn of events would cause him concern. I told him that Mabel knows nothing, nothing more than you can read on the pamphlet and anyway with such a condition as the 'find a wife' clause it is not surprising that heads might be turned occasionally. Torben replied that it was all very well meeting people along the way and talking to them but someone who tags along over a period of time might hear something that they shouldn't and I must not forget that I have a history of recklessness and erratic behaviour which has got me into deep trouble before. He cautioned me to be extremely careful and not under any circumstances reveal my real identity to Mabel as I knew so little about her and her motives. I said that she was sure to quickly tire of the journey as it was so arduous, especially for a lady.

Torben asked to see the perambulator and I put on my silk mask and took him downstairs to a store room where the perambulator was drying out after the day's deluge. The undercarriage was very loose and one of the wheels was no longer a proper circle. It was definitely time to buy a better version. I put it to him that as he was taking half the money and had in fact financed all the equipment at the start it was only right and proper that he should pay for the new perambulator. I was expecting a discussion, ending with us agreeing to split the cost half and half but to my surprise he agreed to stump up the full amount, even when I said it should be made to my design.

Later that evening there was a second knock on my door. It was Mabel.

Potion

Portsmouth, February 20, 1908

'It's an ugly machine.'

That was Torben's verdict on the new perambulator. I would admit that I had sacrificed beauty for practicality but these are the lessons of daily toil. I knew from experience what was required and I had it designed and built. The pneumatic bicycle tyres were what I most desired and they were not easily accommodated as they were so large that they required the axles to be different widths otherwise they would not have fitted the chassis, or the perambulator would have needed to be twice as long. It was a very striking design which to me demonstrated a strength of purpose and I was sure that was how it would be perceived by the public. It had a canopy of soft leather at each end which completely closed up in the centre so that our merchandise could be protected in inclement weather. It was no beauty but at last I would be free of the numbing vibrations of the road.

Despite Torben's discouraging remarks the machine photographs well and I am looking forward to getting back on the road after three days laid up in Portsmouth.

Torben is also greatly annoyed because Mabel has been my constant companion. I have greatly enjoyed her company and conversation. Albert is a taciturn sort and ran out of stimulating talk about the same time that we crossed the Thames, our conversations revolve around the practical these days and whatever charms Albert does have, he certainly cannot compete with the flirtatious and vivacious Miss Reed.

We made one of our customary theatre appearances in a break between performances at the Theatre Royal and although Mabel stayed on the sidelines there was much speculation as to her identity. I said it would be best if she did not reveal her name as the press would make so much of it and so she introduced herself as a Sussex lady to anyone who enquired.

As we prepared to move on the weather took a turn back to winter and thick snowflakes began to fall. Mabel said that she was going back to her home but we arranged to meet up again in a fortnight in Weymouth.

The machine was in tiptop condition, which was just as well as we now faced some of the most trying conditions on the walk so far. The snow was thick and sucked at the wheels making pushing the perambulator very arduous indeed. The nights were cold and turned the soft snow to sharp ice, meaning that the ruts were hard and unforgiving and there was danger in every step. We slipped and tripped our way through Southampton and then the New Forest. The weather did not relent and if it were not for my rendezvous I would gladly have encamped in a warm hostelry. The perambulator was excellent throughout, a machine that was engineered for the task and I was pleased that I had discarded the previous model which would likely have fallen apart under these demanding conditions.

All the time when I was not stumbling I was lost in thought about Mabel. She had spent all three nights with me in Portsmouth and I longed to see her again in Weymouth but I was so conflicted. What about my Kate, waiting for me in Thetford? Even though her letters had offered no support for my venture, she has my children and she had taken my money, which was a small token of recognition of my efforts. All the time in prison I had longed for a reconciliation but I now despaired that she would not join me. That being said I would rather not be where I am, knee deep in snow and ice and chilled as if I were a halibut on a fishmonger's slab but her nagging about my coming home and being a proper family is constant, when in Thetford my income would be pennies instead of the pounds that I'm earning now. It makes no sense.

Mabel makes sense. She's a lady with clear vision, she knows what she wants and she is ready to strive to achieve it. Who am I to stand in her way? I can have a wife for the road. Why not?

Because I am already married. Because I have done this before and it all ended calamitously. Because I promised Kate I would keep out of trouble.

I failed to keep out of trouble when I opened my bedroom door to Mabel. That promise is over but whatever happens I must not marry again. If I was ever unmasked that would be the end of me.

Mabel asks me over and over for my name and is somewhat taken aback when she hears Torben call me farmer boy, a habit he has not been able to break even though it conflicts with my aristocratic accent. I have put her off the scent of my background by suggesting that he calls me this because of the number of farms my family oversee, so the lies are already piling up and I think it is time for another alias. Perhaps Mr Mason can be dusted off once more. We could use that in public as it is known not to be my name but what about when we are alone? She has seen some of my monogrammed handkerchiefs and knows my initials. It is time to be a Henry again but Henry what? It can't be Burrell or Barker, that might come back to haunt me should I be unmasked. So I need something new, the same but different, Bensley, a name that resembles Bensley?

Never have I been so glad to hear the bark of dogs and feel the press of the crowd of children as when we entered Weymouth, this little seaside gem of a town. To my eye even the most blasted eyesore would be a gem of a town if Mabel were in it, which just goes to show the power of separation. The weather had relented, the snow turned to slush and then melted away which gave us the opportunity to walk with greater speed. The perambulator now freed from the dragging snow, rolls with grace along the road and the only numbness I feel in my hands is due to the cold.

We sing and dance as we roll along the streets to the sea front, selling postcards, photographs and pamphlets in great number. It seems my mood is infectious as everyone is joining in and we make a merry procession. The Mayor is ready in his finest robes and I hug him warmly as if he is my oldest friend whom I haven't set eyes on for years. He holds his gold chain with a worried expression as if not entirely sure of my motives. I break off and take Albert in my hands and as we jig along the promenade, other people lining the streets join in, as if we have all taken some fantastic potion that makes everyone happy.

That potion is Mabel, she is going to be my road wife, a secret ceremony, just Mabel and I and a promise to become Mr and Mrs Iron Mask when the time is right. No paperwork, no witnesses, no consequences. The road winds on forever.

Acclaim

Penzance, April 3, 1908

Here comes another one with his notebook and his hand outstretched, oh yes I am really pleased to meet you too, I hope you have some interesting questions for me as the usual ones are getting so tiresome now. You can call me Mr Mason as Mr Iron Mask is rather a mouthful. That name obviously is not mine as you may recall that I was arrested in Bexleyheath. You don't? Do I have to tell you everything, whatever happened to basic research? I will take some tea and a toasted muffin, would you care for some, of course you would. It's on my account.

The arrest? Of course I will tell you about the arrest but before that you probably want some details about this adventure, this pamphlet sets out the conditions and the route and you can take it with you for reference. Please do not make a direct copy as we sell these along with our other merchandise to pay our way.

We arrived yesterday afternoon. The Golden Lion Inn here in Penzance is a really excellent hotel and proprietor Mr Martin and his splendid staff are very attentive to our needs, the beds are soft and comfortable and the breakfast sets you up for a long day's walk. Not today though, today we will be visiting the town. You have a photographer outside? My assistant and I will be glad to pose after this interview.

Where are we going? We will be leaving tomorrow, probably between 9 and 10 am, just so I know how far is the reach of your paper? Cornwall and Devon, in that case we plan to pass through Camborne, Redruth and on to Launceston, before heading off through North Devon.

The wager? The wager came about because I was in my club in London, I dare not state which one in case someone was to look into which members had not recently visited, when I heard a wealthy American gentleman state categorically that no Englishman could walk around the world anonymously (every time I say this it seems more and more unlikely but you reporters just lap it up). I took up the challenge there and then. The amount is one hundred thousand dollars. Yes, there is a forfeit. I stand to lose five thousand pounds should I not complete the challenge.

No, as you can see I don't wear the mask indoors, I had this garment made to allow me to eat. The goggles? They are a bit alarming aren't they but practical. Yes, I have ventured outside without my mask, in fact on one occasion I went to a barber's shop for a cut and shave and all the clientele were talking about the man in the iron mask. They did not recognise me and I left as quickly as I could.

The mask is here under my seat, do you want to try it on? Yes, it is rather heavy isn't it? Four and a half pounds since you ask. I won't put the padlock on or you will never get it off. I use the straps from my satchels to rest the mask on my shoulders otherwise it can rub excessively. You are right it can be a bit stuffy in there. Maybe walking in the tropics will be difficult but I shall try to avoid the midday sun. I have travelled extensively across India and the Far East so I am prepared for the extremes.

Some people have tried to see my face. Every time I stay in a hotel I have to lock the door and we ask the staff to knock before entering. Once a maid entered and I did not have the mask on and for a second I could see her in a mirror, however I was quick to react and covered my face before it was too late. Another person grabbed at my silk mask but I was ready for him and quickly had him by the throat. Others have wrestled with the helmet but it is securely padlocked as you can see.

The perambulator weighs over a hundredweight. I had it made to my specification recently with bicycle tyres. The previous one wouldn't stand the wear and tear but this is much more robust.

Find a wife? It does seem very odd but you should know that I have had many hundreds of letters with proposals of marriage already, some from titled ladies. I am pleased to say that I recently met a lovely lady from Sussex and we married in a secret ceremony. Mrs Mason is accompanying me around the country but she does not walk, we meet up from time to time along the route.

The court case? Of course, I was arrested for not having a pedlar's license and I used the nom de plume 'Mr H. Mason'. They allowed me to keep my helmet on in court and legal history was made. So that's why I have adopted the name Mr Mason.

How long will it all take? Firstly there is no time limit on the task but as long as I remain fit and healthy and continue to walk at the same rate, some days I can walk fifteen, twenty, even twenty-five miles as long as the weather does not hold me back, so I would hope to finish in 1916.

The sale of the postcards and pamphlets is our only income, we must subsist on the money that we make from these activities. I am a wealthy individual but have no access to my income at this time. Once the walk is over I intend to donate the wager to charity. I support my wife as well, I am allowed to give her up to five hundred pounds every year from my own income for her expenses but during the walk she may not give me even so much as a handkerchief without me paying for it.

I hate talking to these reporters but it can be so much fun, sometimes I can sound as if I am a saint.

I go back to my bedroom where Mabel helps me to take off the silk mask and put on my satchels and don the helmet. My shoulders ache with the burden, an unforgiving pain. Albert joins us in the hotel reception with the perambulator beautifully oiled and polished. Outside there is already a large crowd and two photographers from the press. The first wants a picture of just the two of us, the second wants a picture with the perambulator. Then the proprietors of the hotel emerge and the press photographer asks for a final picture. I shake hands with Mr Martin while Albert greets Mrs Martin. Mabel stands to one side and is looking after the proprietors' young child. We stand stock still staring down the brass lens and then begin the serious business of selling our wares.

Crowds follow our every step as we move from tavern to tavern. I march with as much bearing as I can muster pushing the perambulator determinedly despite the yells and catcalls of the loafers and hangers-on. Albert engages with those who wish to purchase the merchandise. When we would get inside a tavern sometimes we could lose some of the more vociferous members of the crowd to the attractions of the bar but we would always collect more wastrels along the way. It is a trying way to earn money, even if it is mighty profitable. On these days I long for country roads, the wide spaces and freedom to be myself, yet I sometimes have entirely the opposite view when the loneliness of the road sets in and I wish to be back in a town enjoying the sound of coins tinkling into Albert's leather caddy and the promise of an evening with Mabel.

Bounty

I swear if I don't watch that boy every waking moment those horses will be lost. I told Will to use the feedbags but the lazy blighter just throws the food on the floor by the van. Portas has eaten it all and poor Athos does not get a look in. They will both die if Will carries on being this careless. Athos from starvation and Portas will explode. I don't know why Mabel does not keep Will in check because I cannot be with the van all the time, I have to walk after all.

Mind you, she has not been herself these last few days. Talking to the Mayor in that way, most concerning, she nearly told him her proper name and that would never do. Mrs Mason or Mrs Iron Mask, no first names or any other clues, those are the rules. She does get carried away when we are in conversation, dropping hints to where she is from and she has not my eye for the details. I can't cover for it, so I have taken to spinning some larger tales to draw the eye. The last reporter left convinced he had recognised me as a writer for the sport pages of a daily in London and advised me not to be so indiscreet. Idiot!

It is a nuisance though, this bounty on my head. One of the papers says that there is an offer of a hundred pounds for anyone who can unmask me and there are plenty of ruffians ready to try their luck. Now that we have the van I thought that things would get better. Every time we stayed in a hotel it seemed as though we were playing cat and mouse with the staff and I tired of always being on my guard against being unmasked. When we fell on the idea of having a van with horses I thought it would solve this particular irritation and give me a place where I could rest away from the public eye but no such luck! The caravan is just a place where the public can come and watch me at all times of the day and night. A man has to have some privacy which is impossible with a van. Taking my ablutions can be most undignified with a crowd of curious onlookers.

Mabel thinks the van is a pretty little thing and she keeps it all neat and tidy. It has to be because it is so cramped. We cook outside by a camp fire which lacks basic privacy so I have to take my meals inside the van. On top of this Mabel has not been herself recently as she has a sickly pallor and some shortness of breath. I worry about her stamina.

The money still keeps rolling in and Torben always has us in his vision. His investment has paid off many times. He is richer by nearly five hundred pounds and many is the time I have pointed this out to him and asked him how much longer he will be requiring his share, to which he replies how much longer will I continue. I say I would go on longer if I did not have such a drain on my income. He says that I would not have any pennies in my pocket now if were not for his efforts and anyway, he is not the only person who is a drain on my income. It is an impasse. We both wait for the other to move first.

Torben is right that I do spend my money quickly. He continues to bring letters with offers of marriage which I have stopped reading. The only letter I wish for is from Kate but it is never anything more than an acknowledgement of the money I have sent. I send some pounds to Kate every month to make sure that she can give the children some treats. I no longer ask her to join me, though I do think about her a lot and desperately wish that she was here. I realise that Kate understands me better than I do, certainly better than Mabel does, because Kate knows the real me.

With Mabel, I have told her a proper tale of being an aristocrat, I feel bad that I have not told her the truth but I have learnt that Mabel is indiscreet, so it is better for those that overhear her indiscretions that they have no veracity. At the same time I have no rest. In my mind and my actions I must always be the rich aristocrat, with no one can I let down my guard. Therefore I am forever considering my next comment and my next move to make sure it is what Mabel needs to see and hear.

What do I need to hear? The sound of heavy coin in Albert's caddy has been my joy for the last few months. I look at Albert, he has been a faithful man, he has worked as hard as I and his face is lined and weathered and I wonder if I have aged too. I rarely see my own face, not to look at and study. It is as hidden from me as it is from the rest of the world.

Angels

Thetford, June 16, 1908

I am feeling right at home now that I've seen the first flint stone houses on the road into the old town. Here I am walking past Hubbard's field. No haystacks today thank goodness, though I might have set one alight just for old time's sake because I feel so strangely uplifted. Maybe a song will come to my lips but it would give me away should I come out with one of those old farming songs. They would remember me for a local and have me unmasked quick as a flash. Whatever happens some will remember me, so it's a good thing that the reward is no longer news, or I could have trouble here.

Another good thing is that I sent Mabel on to Diss. No one here would take kindly to seeing me with a different wife. Kate's well liked around these parts and I still love her dearly but Mabel would put people's noses out of joint and no mistake, especially now she's sure that she is with child. All that sickness and tiredness and wanting to stay on a van turned out to be the oldest reason of all. I'm glad I told Mabel that she should cut Thetford and go directly to Diss where she can rest for the day, even if it does mean that she can have another day at the shops. It sometimes seems to me that I walk and sell postcards purely to maintain Mabel, Torben, Albert, Will and the horses with no pleasures for myself.

It all seems so familiar, even the faces of the children following the perambulator resemble people I was at school with. That boy there, he reminds me of my brother, I suppose he could even be a nephew. I had better stay quiet, just hearing all these familiar voices and accents makes me want to chime in.

People are recognising Albert though. This plan of mine to come through Thetford is fraught. It's only six months since we left and those who aided me before can't help but remember me. There's a reporter from the Thetford and Watton Times listening nearby and he's eyeing Albert to ask him all about the walk. I bring Albert close in and tell him to keep it quiet. We don't know who is listening in with interested ears and ideas of spoiling our parade. We have to take care. Albert does not look too happy but I know he is looking forward to going home and seeing his wife and children.

Thetford. What purpose did I think would be served by returning here?

I take a room in the Bell Inn. I tell Albert that we are not going to promenade and sell our wares this evening. Due to fatigue I am determined to stay in my room and take a long bath, something that because of the toilet facilities of the caravan I have been missing more often. Albert is going to stay at his home for the evening and I urge him to be cautious regarding his conversations.

The dusk still glows a dim red when I venture out late in the evening but it is no shepherd's delight as I am avoiding the townspeople on my way to knock on Kate's door. I stand and wonder but not for long because the door opens quietly and I am ushered into the kitchen. Kate stands by the range, her hands by her side clenching and unclenching while she glowers at me, a furious beauty. It doesn't matter to me because I still love her.

'Please would it be possible for me to see Alice and Lily?' I say but Kate says nothing, breathing hard, then nods and leads me up the tight staircase to the upper floor. In the back room there are two beds and two golden haired angels are sleeping quietly in the comfort of childhood. My eyes moisten.

'Can I, can I say hello?'

In the darkness I can feel Kate's stare. 'They don't know you.'

In one of the beds an angel stirs, her golden tresses ripple and then her eyes open. It's Alice, little Alice, her face longer than I remember, though she is as pretty as a flower. Alice peers at me through heavy lidded eyes, then Kate and then back to me.

'Mam?'

'I'm here Alice, dear.'

'Who's this, mam?'

There is a long and potent silence. I hold my breath and wait for Kate to unveil me.

'You don't know him but he knows you Alice, very well.'

Alice smiles sleepily. I kneel down beside her bed, caress her rosy pink cheek with my hand, then lean forward and kiss my daughter's forehead. Kate takes my other hand and leads me away from the bedroom and back down the tight staircase to the kitchen.

'What have you come here for?' Kate stands by the hearth with her arms folded, her fingers round her waist holding her body tightly.

'I came to see how you and my daughters are faring. I did not think I would have to walk so far to see you again.'

Her eyes flashed angrily.

'Don't lay this on me Harry Bensley, that's your choice. I didn't send you away, you took this foolish challenge all by yourself. You know my mind, I've not wavered.'

'I have sent you money.'

'Money! You have that and we need it Harry. I'll accept your money because without it I wouldn't have this home to keep your children safe. Money is a help and no mistake but it is not all that we need, I need you. Alice and Lily need you. You carry on with this folly as if it is a little excursion. It's no holiday for us, while you are out there, we are still here living our lives and Alice and Lily are growing up. You miss out on that while you tramp around the world on your foolish challenge. Is it worth it Harry?'

'That money is hard earned, Kate, every single day that I am on the road I make more money than I can earn toiling in the fields around here for a month. If I stayed here would you have this little house? I don't think so, we would struggle, we would be poor.'

'We, what we? Do you think I don't struggle every day without you here at my side to help me? Money is all very well but money does not light the hearth, money does not comfort Lily when she has a nightmare, money does not make me any less lonely.'

'Then why did you not join me when I asked you.'

'That's just ridiculous Harry and you know it. How could I with two young girls to look after? How can we go gallivanting around the countryside with no proper home and no schooling for Alice and Lily? They have their friends as well, Alice is nine and a proper clever little girl who loves her schooling and Lily is devoted to her big sister. You've never seen it Harry, 'cause you've never been here to witness your family.'

'I wanted us to be a family all together on the road.'

'That's just fool's talk, Harry. There is nothing I long for more than for us to be together but what have I always said to you? If we are together then we have no secrets and no lies. When you go away you start your fibbing and those fibs get bigger and bigger. I won't join you on the road because it is one great big lie and I don't tell lies. Until you start seeing the truth in that, I won't have you back neither.'

'Is that your last word?'

'No Harry, I'm not finished yet. You may not know it but you are a notable person and they write stories about you in the newspapers. They often talk about you needing a wife and they say sometimes that you are married. Have you got married again Harry? Are you so shanny that you'd risk the gaoler's knock?'

'I haven't actually married.'

'I know you Harry, that's not an answer. I said I read the papers, I see she travels in a van with you.'

'She's not here.'

'No and I wouldn't want to meet her anyhow, or more to the point, perhaps you would prefer it if she didn't know about me. I thought so, your face is an open book to me, Harry. I don't know what you are doing but I'll pray for you. One day this is going to be over and you will need me, you know you will.'

Parsimony

Ludlow, September 3, 1908

'A temperance hotel Henry, really? Is this some low jibe?'

'Nothing of the sort but things being what they are we must cut our cloth to suit, Mabel.'

'Cut your own cloth, Henry. I have my allowance to do with as I wish and I will tell you now I do not wish to stay in a temperance hotel with a crowd of earnest Christians. If I had wanted that I would have stayed with my parents.'

'That's all very well but funds are not what they were and during the last couple of weeks walking from the Welsh border I have not realised as much as I would have hoped. The weather has been a complete hindrance, thunderstorms, high winds and that last deluge nearly washed both Albert and me away. People are staying indoors and can you blame them? I do not wish to be out in this tempest either, the helmet cuts me so and I have such aches and pains all exacerbated by the numbing cold but despite all of that we had this rendezvous, so here I am and I am sorry this isn't the Ritz but things will change when we get into the Midland counties. We made a few pounds on the town promenade today at least.'

'Change? What will change, Henry? Are you going to stop walking? No, that won't change. It's such a bore, moving here, moving there, just a couple of days stopping to see the mayor and the press and then we're off. It's interminable. It's all right for you, you're doing the damned walk but I get pestered everywhere I go by nosy little louts and then there are the women, oh they go on and on about how do I do this, what do I think about that and they are forever asking difficult and pointed questions such as where are we going to live when this is finished. Some of those women can tell, they can just tell

I am pregnant. I don't know if they have a sixth sense or what and they keep on and on even though I deny it. I can't keep denying it, soon even the most short-sighted old coot's going to know. You're not listening, are you? I wish you would take that stupid hat and goggles off, you look like a frog in mourning.'

'I have to keep them on darling, you never know when someone might open the door.'

'Oh you are listening, well there's a surprise. So what about me, Henry? Now that the van's gone and I'm at the mercy of the railways. What about me? It's lonely out there travelling from town to town, waiting for you.'

'The van had to go. We agreed it was costing too much to keep it on the road and that young Will was a liability. Anyway with the weather turning it would be terribly cramped. What about poor Albert? Stuck under canvas in the winter.

'You think about Albert's comfort but what about me and my comforts? It's not easy getting about, especially in my condition.'

'Maybe it is time for you to go back home.'

'What?'

'Maybe you should go back to your family and have the baby. Then once things are better, we can get back together again.'

'So you want me to leave?'

'I don't understand Mabel, you've read the pamphlet many times, it does not say I can take time off to care for my family. What I want is to make you as comfortable as possible and if that means going back to your family home, then so be it but we will get back together soon.'

'On the road?'

'Yes.'

'With a baby?'

'With our baby, yes.'

'Henry, I don't want to go back to my parents. Why can't I go and stay in your home? After all that you've told me about your family they could give up a wing of it and barely notice I was there. Then there will be your servants and I could have a nanny and all the best care. It would be so much more comfortable for me and our baby.'

'I cannot do that, unfortunately.'

'Why not Henry, what is stopping you from letting me stay at the Old Manor House?'

'It's just that they don't know that I am the Iron Mask.'

'They don't know! How can they not know? That is ridiculous, Henry.'

'No, it's entirely possible because they are country people and they don't move in the same circles as I did when I lived in London, so I didn't tell them I was taking part in this challenge. They think I am in New Zealand working as an importer, exporter. Truth be told and I think you need to know this Mabel, my father gave me an allowance and I lost everything in a card game and this challenge rather came out of that. If my parents were to find out I was here it would be disastrous for me. Not only would I forfeit my allowance but my standing in society as well. The only way for me to recover my reputation and my wealth is to fulfil this challenge. If you were to appear at the door of my father's estate not only would he bring this whole enterprise to a halt by unmasking me and forcing me home, he would also not care and indeed relish the opportunity to finish my reputation as a gentleman in London society. We would be paupers amongst plenty, always waiting for a handout from my father and you could wait a terribly long time for that.'

'A card game, I've never seen you so much as look at a pack of cards, what nonsense is this?'

'It's true that I foreswore all games of chance afterwards but that is because I lost my allowance on the turn of a card.'

'So you would send me back to my home because your father would ruin you?'

'He would not just ruin me, he would ruin us. In the past he has reluctantly paid up my gambling debts but this wager is too large. It is my whole allowance, forever. He won't pay that out to someone else.

It is more likely he would put me in a labourer's cottage and have me milking the cows from dawn to dusk.'

'What about my allowance, my five hundred pounds per annum?'

'You will have it once I have won this wager but until then the money is coming out of the income on the road and sometimes there isn't any, not enough to speak of, anyway.'

'So these ten pounds that you have given me?'

'Indeed I have just earned it.'

'And I have spent it.'

'Yes, that does seem to be the way of it, you have adapted rather well to your newly acquired wealth. It's a shame really as it could be helpful now.'

'But I took you at your word.'

'And I have every intention of making good your allowance but things are tight. Once we reach those Midland cities the money will be rolling in. Look Mabel, you can have all that I've got, we took over six pounds today and I'll send more money on, then once you've had the baby and are ready, we'll be back on the road again, this time with a bigger van for you and our child. I promise you that and when has the Mask ever failed, eh?'

'I will be miserable without you.'

'I will too but this will be for the best.'

'You will send me money?'

'Every week, I promise.'

'I don't want to be away from you.'

'Me neither but this is for the best, I promise.'

Severance

Leicester, October 14, 1908

My dearest Kate,

I wave to you from fair Leicester and hope this letter finds you and Lily and Alice well.

Since I last wrote we have walked through much of the central and eastern counties of the midlands. Right now I am staying in a hotel in the city and though it's not of the highest quality it does at least have a decent hot bath in which to salve the aches and pains. The weather has not been the best as autumn catches hold with its blustery winds and wet downpours but that is only to be expected as the seasons change. I plan to stay here for a couple of days as the music hall has extended an invitation to present myself during the performance tomorrow evening.

I have some sad news about young Albert although maybe you have already heard. He had sorely missed his family and as the weather had tumbled into autumn his mood darkened with the clouds. It came to a head while we walked through Peterborough and were approached by a mother with a gaggle of children that struck young Albert as a mirror of his own family and he could not shake off the desire to leave my service and see them again. He sobbed and said he was sorry to let me down but he was handing in his caddy as it was his strong desire to return to his wife and children.

Of course I was flabbergasted but I had no option but to set him free. I gave him a decent severance as he has been an honest and hard-working assistant and I fully respect his reasons for stopping. I fear though that for me this walk is hard enough with company but to face it alone is a much greater obstacle.

A couple of days ago I met with Torben. I look forward to seeing him because of course he is the conduit of our correspondence. I used to think he was a decent fellow, especially when we were confederates at his majesty's pleasure but I find his company irksome these days. He pokes his nose into every detail, counting the stock, asking about the amount of time spent walking around the town. Have we approached the music halls? How much did we take here, why did we not take more money there? It just goes on and on. Then he takes his share of the income. He has made back his initial investment a hundred-fold but he still comes back for more. When I complain, he reminds me that without his help and particular assistance especially in Bexleyheath during the court case I would not have achieved any of this so it is only right that he takes his due. He does do work for his portion, he makes sure that I am always stocked up with photographs and pamphlets. If I had to do all that as well I don't believe I would achieve any distance at all but the unspoken fact is that we both know that the takings are going down. The Iron Mask is no longer a novelty, although the money is still fair and it is actually a help that Albert has left us as it means one less mouth to feed. I am enclosing as much money as I can for you and the children in the hope that it will keep you warm and fed until Christmas.

I did discuss with Torben the idea of finding another assistant but he was not in favour of it as he reasoned that our income is insufficient. I pointed out that if he was to consider reducing his share it would make an assistant easier to afford but he just laughed and said I needed him more than I needed an assistant. It is true that I needed him once but I believe he is a heavy burden these days.

I do not wish to complain about my lot but the journey is taking its toll. The perambulator was always heavy to push and the cause of aches on my arms and torso. I did think it would get better but the pains either move about or change in nature from stabbing to throbbing. The worst thing though is the helmet which is a constant rub on my neck and shoulders. My muscles ache from the weight and I have to bear terrible headaches daily. Every evening a bath is imperative to calm my muscles and warm my bones and sleep, when I can achieve it is a welcome respite.

I miss the company of Albert even though the two of us may not have conversed much but his mere presence was a great comfort. I miss him most when a crowd of rowdy townsfolk surround me on the road. Although mostly their conversation is light-hearted and jovial, occasionally some fellow's countenance will darken as he witnesses the purchase of my wares. I fear for my goods, the purse and indeed my person on these occasions and although so far I have managed to walk unmolested, I do wonder just how much longer it will be before some ruffian takes his chance. In anticipation of such an eventuality I have recently purchased a baton to use in self-defence.

I wish I could hear something of your news. I miss those mornings when I would walk down to Hubbard's field and wave to you in your room, or when we would meet in the church on a Sunday and spend the afternoon in the summer sun walking along the river. It is always sunny in my memory. I am still the same man, I still love you dearly Kate and I miss you more than any written word can say.

The plan for the next fortnight is that from Leicester I intend to walk to Coventry where Torben has already arranged that I will be presented to the Mayor and also visit the Hippodrome Theatre. Then on to Birmingham to promenade for a few days and next to Wolverhampton where I have an engagement at the Empire Palace Theatre on the 25th October.

Please do write to me.

Your ever loving husband,

Harry.

Kate's kitchen – 4

Thetford, November, 1908

'That's the truth of it Kate, the whole truth of it as it happened.'

'We can't tell people that Harry, they will come looking for you.'

'I know but you want me to write this article and it has to be true.'

'True, yes but there are parts of your tale that are better left untold.'

'I know exactly what you mean, so to finish up.

Since then I have been wearing this helmet daily for ten months, a weight of four pounds and five ounces. I have wheeled the perambulator which weighed one hundredweight and one pound, a distance of two thousand and four hundred miles. The strain began to tell upon me. My eyes ached and I suffered with racking pains to my head. On several occasions I fainted by the roadside and sometimes I was confined to my bed for two or three days at a stretch. It was then that my wife insisted that I should give up the walk. I should like to have continued with it but circumstances were too strong for me. I had to cancel arrangements that I had made to appear at several music halls when I left Wolverhampton a few weeks ago.

In conclusion, I can assert without fear of contradiction that I have paid my way and supported myself, my wife and my assistant, the horses and attendants entirely from the sale of my cards and pamphlets and that I have received nothing in the shape of charity from the first day of the itinerary.

Kate stopped reading the article in Answers magazine and put the paper down on the kitchen table. Harry sat motionless on a kitchen chair staring into the spitting flames of the range fire. Finally he stood up and enveloped Kate in his arms.

'You have no idea how liberating it is to finally tell it all. I feel it will be fine, dearest Kate. It will all be fine.'

The Galloping Major (slight refrain)

Or Whatever happened to Harry's wives?

I don't tell ev'ryone but still,
I was married some time ago.
I regret of the matter to speak.
We were only together a week.
I endeavoured, of course, to make Gwendoline happy,
But one day, alas! And alack!
That impulsive young creature ran home to her mother,
And said that she wouldn't come back.
I decried that I thought it was rough,
She replied that she'd had quite enough,
Bumpety, bumpety, bumpety, bump ...

Beach

Clacton-on-Sea, August bank holiday weekend, 1933

'Good morning, Mr Bensley sir, would you like a hand with that?'

'Most kind of you William, thank you, you're always here in a timely manner.'

'You're early sir, the sun is barely above the pier and it's going to be a sparkler, the needle on the barometer is set to fine, the tide is out at midday so there'll be plenty of beach for the kiddies. I notice we've got five holiday specials due in from London and the Midlands all full to bursting and there's several steamers docking up at the pier this morning. Should be a brisk day for you sir, on the promenade.'

'I hope so William, be careful with the old lady mind, she's seen better days.'

'She's a fine old machine, she's taken you around the world and by the looks of her she'd do it again.'

'The spirit's willing but my legs don't have the vim these days. Up and down the promenade is as far as I want to go. So I can plan my day William, what time does the last of the specials leave?'

'Seven o'clock.'

'I'll be back for the train after, William.'

'That'll be the seven-seventeen to Liverpool Street, I'll see you then Mr Bensley, sir.'

'I'll just set my watch by the station clock.'

'The one by the ticket office carries the latest London time, sir.'

--

'Can I see your pedlar's license?'

'You never tire of that do you Constable Gammons?'

'That would be a day for my notebook that one and no mistake Mr Bensley. It's always in order I know, because I gave it to you but I have to ask.'

'What would you do if I had forgotten it?'

'Oh, don't you start Mr Bensley, sir. That would be a laugh wouldn't it just? I would march you back to court with your helmet on. Let's have another go and see what the bench says this time. Honestly though, we'd sort it out between us, it would be no problem just don't make it a habit.'

'I haven't so far and I have no intention in the future.'

'Have a good day sir, it's going to be a scorcher.'

—

'Did you do it?'

'Madam?'

'I remember seeing you as a young girl when I lived in Worthing. It must have been when I was seven. We were walking through the town and there was this tremendous bustle and fanfare and in the middle of it all was you and this pram. I still remember it as clear as day. I badgered my father for a tanner to buy one of your postcards. So did you do it? I've long thought about you. Did you win the wager?'

'I got a long way, madam.'

'But you didn't do it?'

'I strongly wish that I had completed it madam, but alas, I did not win the wager.'

'So what happened, what stopped you?'

'The war happened madam. I would have won the wager but my country's need was greater than mine.'

'Oh, that was, let's see, six years later so tell me more, where were you when the war broke out? You must have got a long way.'

'Yes, madam, I had indeed nearly completed the itinerary. In fact I had just landed in Genoa when I was informed of the outbreak of the War. I only had to complete the European leg but even if I had wanted to continue that was of course impossible. As it was I returned to join the army but I was soon invalided out. It was hard at the front.'

'What a story, what a story and what a shame. However I will buy a postcard for my children. They're out on the sands building sandcastles with their father. Look see over there, there they are, waving. I wonder if I still have the old one. I'm sure I pasted it into one of my scrap books. I shall get it out and frame it. You're an inspiration of the best kind, a heroic failure.'

'That's most kind of you madam, a shilling if you please, thank you.'

——

'Still taking the money, farmer boy?'

'Torben. What a surprise! What brings you down here?'

'It was a little article in the London Evening News. I read it and I thought, this sounds familiar but then maybe not, because the man in this article travels so much further than I remember, so maybe he is not the same man but someone who does something similar. It is you though, is it not?'

'I may have added some miles to my tale.'

'So I am correct because I got to thinking that this man that I knew, he was quite an imaginative man and maybe he could be my old friend. But then I also think he tells me he has to stop telling lies because his wife told him to stop, so maybe he is no longer with his wife and he can go back to being the way he was.'

'You know me better than anyone, Torben.'

'The article I read says that this man is often to be found on the beach front in Clacton. So I think to myself that for my next holiday I will take the sea air because it is good for me and maybe I will meet up with an old friend and see how he is going.'

'It has been twenty-five years, Torben.'

'Twenty-five years and look, you have not changed. You still push a pram for a living. I hear that now you tell people that you have pushed that pram a long way, so how far do you say you go?'

'I tell them I walked until the outbreak of the war.'

'That was what the newspaper said. You stopped to join the army and then were invalided out, it makes you sound as if you are a hero.'

'It's mainly true, I did join the army, the packers and loaders in Aldershot but I pulled my back and they discharged me after only three months.'

'It is mainly true, only the Harry Bensley I know could say that! And what a glorious war, Harry.'

'What happened to you?'

'During the war?'

'Since we last parted.'

'Ah, you want to hear my truth. That was in Wolverhampton wasn't it. I have dark memories of the town, the rain, the cold. Meeting your wife, your real wife that is and being told by her what you are going to do. She ruined my plans you know.'

'She wanted it to end and she wanted me to tell the truth in that article.'

'End? Why end it? I could have found another iron mask. I could have continued with it. It still made money.'

'Not enough.'

'How can you say that, we made several fortunes.'

'You did. I barely kept my head above water.'

'And whose fault was that, farmer boy? I did not make you give five hundred pounds to a 'wife'. I did not make you hire horses and a caravan while you also stayed in fine hotels. No, what I did was make sure you always had enough stock to sell and places to sell it. Everything I did was to enrich you but you found ways to spend it even quicker.'

'I went back to my wife because it was over, I could go no further.'

'Yes, you went back with your wife, after all that time she takes you back. You are an easy man to like, Harry but I think I can only feel sorrow for those who love you. It did not last, I think, your marriage?'

'No, I loved Kate but I could not live with her always telling me what to do, so after I joined the army I did not go back home. So tell me, what happened to you after that?'

'I met a lady and married, we had two children, two boys, all was good and then the war happened. As a German citizen I was rounded up and put in a camp. A dirty draughty nowhere place with high walls and barbed wires. The sentries used to say to us, you are lucky to be in here, you are safe in here but I never felt safe. Soon I stopped getting post from my wife, she did not want to know me anymore, she did not want people to think that she sympathised with a German. Then they moved us, every last one of us, over to the Isle of Man and I was there until 1919. Even so, I do consider myself lucky as if I had been in Germany I would have met the same fate as my brothers who were conscripted into the army and both killed on the same day in April 1918. They were farmers not soldiers, sent to their slaughter by the Kaiser. They let me go once the War was over and I stayed here in Britain, despite the terrible discrimination and abuse. My wife took my fortune and I haven't seen my children since 1914 though I always hope. I have gone back to book-keeping. I sit in a dingy office with six other men and they ignore me. So I daydream, I daydream about prison, can you imagine? And I daydream about us and how we once lived as kings.'

'That is a very sorry tale.'

'Then I saw the article in the newspaper and I thought I would like to talk with you one last time before I go.'

'Before you go? Where are you going?'

'My plan is to travel back to Bavaria, as my father is alone and to keep the farm going is a struggle for him. I will go back and be a farmer boy once more.'

'We are both a little old for that.'

'My father is older. I have given up hoping to see my children so maybe they will come and find me when I go back to Germany and be a bachelor farmer.'

'When will you go?'

'When I have saved enough money for the trip. My pay is meagre and my rent exorbitant. They take advantage of us Germans.'

'How much do you need?'

'Five pounds.'

'Here, I have three.'

'Thank you farmer boy. Giving me money, it is just like old times.'

'Just like old times. Good luck and goodbye, Torben.'

——

'Evening Mr Bensley, sir, do you want a hand with the old lady into the luggage carriage?'

'Thank you, William, that would be most kind.'

'Did you have a good day, sir? It was hot on the beach, wasn't it just?'

'It was a good day for the Rossi ice cream salesmen. I think I would say I had an interesting day, you meet all sorts on the promenade.'

'You do that sir. You do that. Will you be back tomorrow?'

'I don't think I will, tomorrow I fancy I will be in Southend-on-Sea.'

'So is that the end of you this season?'

'Maybe, it depends on when the weather turns. Here's something for your trouble, William and good evening.'

'Thank you sir and safe journey home.'

——

'I'm home, Kate. I've brought a fish and chip supper.'

'All right Harry I'm in the kitchen, there's a bottle of Ridleys cooling on the shelf in the larder for you. How did it go today, my love?'

'Steady, not as good as usual, people come and look at my articles but they just don't have the spare change that they used to.'

'That looks down quite a bit from last year. Is it time to give it a rest?'

'No, not yet, I'll try Southend tomorrow. Anyway it all helps over the winter, I'll put it in the jar.'

'You got a letter this morning. Council business it looks like and the Dock Road people want to know if you will speak at a meeting in the village hall about the new street lamps.'

'Not now love, I'll look it over later.'

'Anything happen today, anything out of the ordinary?'

'Just another day, my love, just another day.'

Postscript

Even fiction comes from truth.
Ridley Scott, 2018

The facts about Harry Bensley

The facts about the Iron Mask

Some assumptions

Acknowledgments

The facts about Harry Bensley

In the plan of his Pennine Way Companion, Alfred Wainwright explains why it has been designed in such a strange manner. For those who have never seen the guide I should explain that the main text is an annotated map and in order to follow it you must start from the back of the book and as Wainwright states, in a manner strange to western ideas, turn each page forward ending at the front. Another bizarre concept is that you read up the page following the route of the Pennine Way from south to north. He explains logically and clearly why he had designed this book in this unusual manner and unless you are actually walking the Pennine Way it will not make any sense. To be honest it still did not make sense when I was using it but stay with me here. The main point is that on page four, i.e., very near the front, there is an essay entitled 'The End' which is intended to be read only by those who complete the challenge. It is a fine essay, although maybe a little dated and slightly sexist to the modern eye as it is unaware of the concept of women walking the Pennine Way but the point I am trying to make is that if you have flicked here first, instead of reading the rest of the book, then what follows is a series of spoilers. Read on if you must but I would suggest that you will enjoy this much more if you read it after the main narrative.

Harry Bensley was born in 1876 in Thetford. His father was also called Harry Bensley and was a sawmill worker. It is not known whether or where he went to school but since it was a legal requirement from 1870 for all children to be taught up to the age of 14 it is a fair assumption that he did.

When he was 14 he left school and started as a shepherd working for the local butcher, Mr Hubbard. According to newspaper reports he was charged with arson following a haystack fire. He was found not guilty.

He next appears in the 1891 Census living at 1 St Giles Lane, Thetford with his parents. He is still a farm labourer.

In 1897 he appears in Thetford Magistrates Court charged with feloniously stealing items of clothing from the Thetford Industrial Co-operative Society and unlawfully obtaining with intent to defraud other clothing items from Henry Webster. He is sentenced on each count to three months hard labour to run concurrently. It is also noted that he had a previous criminal record, having been found guilty of stealing money at Westminster Police Court on the 4th November 1876 and sentenced to six months in prison. This is the only record of this misdemeanour as the original records were lost in the reorganisation that happened during the formation of the London County Council.

The crimes in Thetford occurred two weeks before he was found guilty of stealing money in London. Furthermore his arrest and subsequent court case in Thetford happened a matter of days after his release from prison in the capital. At this moment it can be safely said that he is a criminal but he is certainly no mastermind.

The other point of interest is a column in the court report that is marked 'degree of instruction'. This is an indication of the reading and writing ability of the prisoner and here he is scored as 'Imp'. 'Imp' is generally assumed these days to mean imperfect and suggests that he can read and write but not with any great proficiency.

In 1898 Harry marries Kate Green in Thetford. Kate Green is supposed to have come from Ipswich and is alleged to be an orphan. These facts are open to interpretation as her mother was definitely alive. His first daughter Alice is born in 1899 and his second daughter Lily in 1900. Both are born in Thetford. Harry's occupation during this time is noted as a labourer.

The first mention of the family's move to London is when Harry turns up in the infirmary of Stepney Workhouse where he is admitted for epilepsy on the 25th February 1901. He stays until the 2nd of March. His wife, Kate and two children are noted under the remarks column. His occupation is labourer and it states that he was admitted to the Infirmary from the Workhouse. This does open up a lot of questions but the most interesting one is does Harry Bensley suffer from epilepsy? There is no further evidence for this so I would question the diagnosis. Firstly because it is possible for any one of us to have an epileptic fit once in our lifetime and secondly because a diagnosis of epilepsy these days requires significant and lengthy tests.

The 1901 Census was undertaken on March 31st which is less than four weeks after the workhouse incident and it finds the Bensley family living in 34 Woodbridge Road, South Norwood. It gives Kate's birthplace as Ipswich and Harry is still a general labourer.

Following the records the next event is the marriage of Henry Burrell to Lily Clapham in 1903 at Marylebone Registry Office. Henry Burrell it transpires is one of several aliases that Harry Bensley takes over the next five years. Three or four months later a boy is born but there is no record of the name.

In May 1904, Harry Barker, his wife Lily and child are arrested in Cape Town, South Africa, on charges of fraud, while disembarking from a boat destined for Australia. They are brought back to Britain where the aliases Harry Barker and Henry Burrell are revealed to belong to Harry Bensley. He is charged with fraud and bigamy and the court case takes place in the Old Bailey on the 16th of November 1904 in front of the Common Serjeant, the second highest ranked judge in Britain.

The court records of the trial reveal that Harry pleaded guilty to the fraud but not guilty to bigamy. If he had taken legal advice he would surely have pleaded the other way around but the trial records show that he conducted his own defence. The trial is mainly about the abandonment of his wife Kate, his subsequent relationship and bigamous marriage to Lily Clapham and a series of mysterious attempts to reconnect with his first wife that failed.

Some facts that came out in evidence were that his wife Kate was an orphan. There is no corroborative evidence for this but it seems likely that she considered herself an orphan. In the census records I can find a Kate Green of the right age in Ipswich in 1881 and 1891 but the rest of the family's first names are significantly different, suggesting that she was living with the families of aunts and uncles. There is no record of her in any of the orphanages or workhouses.

Then there is the testimony from Lily Clapham that Harry stated several times that he would commit suicide and indeed made one attempt that does sound very much as if it were a panic attack. Finally as I write in the main narrative, he did call to the stand the policeman George Cole in a strange and desperate attempt to try and bolster his case, to no avail.

The newspaper reports of the time give conflicting details of the fraud and the amounts involved. Whatever the sums actually were the fraud was ruinous for his victims. These reports had little interest in the actual proceedings of the trial and it seems that the articles were written after interviews with his victims.

Confusingly, some of the newspaper reports call Lily, Lily Chapham but I have decided that the Old Bailey transcript is the most likely to be correct. Lily is a most fugitive person, with no record of her birth, one record of her marriage and no census records. The child also disappears, probably into an orphanage or given up for adoption.

Harry Bensley is sentenced to four years penal servitude and sent to Pentonville Prison. In the home office record his degree of instruction which we saw before was 'Imperfect' is now assessed as 'Well' meaning that he was regarded as well-educated and this tells its own story about the effects of the preceding years.

It is difficult to actually know what penal servitude entailed in 1904. The way that prisoners were treated was slowly changing but certainly it is a matter of record that in the latter years of the nineteenth century Pentonville enacted one the harshest prison regimes in the country. Known as the Separate System, it maintained not merely silence but continual separation between the prisoners as they undertook the hard labour. Under that system it would have been impossible for any prisoner to mix with another. Indeed any effort to do so was harshly punished. It is suggested that suicide and madness was common amongst the prisoners. However, by 1904 these were old fashioned ideas and some small changes were occurring. Just how progressive Pentonville Prison was by this date is pure speculation though.

There is no record of Harry Bensley or any of his family in the 1911 Census and there are some who consider this evidence that he is off walking round the world. The next time his name appears on any record is after the outbreak of the Great War.

Harry Bensley joins the army in 1915. The enlistment record shows that he has been working as an attendant in an asylum in Abbots Langley and that his wife is Kate Green. Sometime over the previous eight years he has been reunited with his first wife. He joins the Packers and Loaders company in Aldershot but it doesn't last and he is discharged on medical grounds three months later. He does receive an armlet from the army, the purpose of which is for him to wear to show that he has played his part in the war. At that time it was common for men of enlistment age to be 'shown the white feather' if it was thought they were avoiding their national duty and the armlet was protection against this. The address on the package is unusual as it was not his last place of work but in Catford. According to Dick Barton in 'Wivenhoe – its attractions, pleasures and eccentric natives', Harry then worked as a shell examiner at Woolwich Arsenal.

After the war, Harry and Kate moved to Wivenhoe, an estuary town in Essex. He worked as a commissionaire at a cinema, exploiting his fine voice and aristocratic bearing, as a collector for the Essex Medical Hospital Fund and became a secretary for the Transport and General Workers Union.

He also took the perambulator and knight's helmet to the seafront in Southend-on-Sea and Clacton-on-Sea on sunny weekends and bank holidays when he would parade along the promenade, sell his postcards and tell his story.

While in Wivenhoe, as documented in 'The Story of Wivenhoe' by Nicholas Butler, Harry became a Labour councillor after a failed attempt to become a councillor on a British Legion ticket the year before. He was elected first in 1931 and then lost his seat in 1934 before being re-elected in 1935. It is ironic to find that he had a small part in helping to straighten out the council's finances and balancing the books after a clerk had been found guilty of embezzlement. He is remembered as a maverick with a bizarre notoriety. He would have blended in quite well with modern day Wivenhoe (that's my observation).

Barton suggests that Harry left the town as mysteriously as he arrived just before the outbreak of the second world war, though Butler claims that ill health caused Harry to resign as Councillor in 1936 and leave Wivenhoe, moving first to Sutton, in Surrey.

In the electoral roll records he can be seen to move several times before finally dying in Brighton in 1956. According to the McNaught website his wife Kate was at his side.

The facts about the Iron Mask

It does not matter how you look at this story, nobody knows for certain the identity of the person wearing the Iron Mask on New Year's Day in 1908. That being said there is not a long list of claimants for the role. In fact there is only one and that is Harry Bensley. The genius of his idea (if it was his idea, let's keep an open mind) was that the man in the mask could be anyone and given his ability to mimic an aristocratic accent and weave the illusion of wealth and social standing, the Iron Mask became exactly who his audience wanted him to be.

His travels are extensively recorded. The Daily Mirror was summoned to Trafalgar Square for the start and his story was syndicated across Britain and the world. To be arrested in Bexleyheath the very next day was on the face of it an absolute disaster but as we now know there is no such thing as bad news and the success of the court case in Dartford gave the whole enterprise extra impetus right from the beginning.

This meant that practically every local town paper on the route was poised for the arrival of the man in the mask and many conducted interviews along the way. Most of those interviews were purely restating the terms of the wager but sometimes more interesting tidbits would emerge, for example his move into the music halls to sell his wares, which began in Maidstone and became a regular way to bolster his coffers.

Then there was his 'wife'. He'd hoped that his real wife Kate would join him on the road but we know that she didn't. We don't know why, although having two young daughters might have been part of the problem.

The first mention of his 'wife' occurs in Exeter at the end of March 1908. Many years later the lady in question is claimed to be a Mabel

Reed, born in Sussex in 1870, some six years older than Harry. She had married a Thomas Kemp in 1890 and there is no record of a divorce. In fact her death is recorded in her married name in 1926. The 'Iron Mask' and Mabel are supposed to have married in secret, although it is more likely they would only have committed to marriage once they were free to do so, rather than actually taking part in a ceremony that could have landed them both in prison. In any case there is no record of such an event. Mabel's real name is never used in any newspaper article and where any name is used, she is usually referred to as Mrs Iron Mask.

In Penzance, the Iron Mask was photographed with his new 'wife'. The next time her presence is recorded by the press she is living in a 'van', a horse drawn caravan that follows him around.

By the beginning of May, having walked nearly a thousand miles, Mr and Mrs Iron Mask as they are described, are having tea with the Mayor of Reading in their caravan and taking interviews with journalists. There are occasional hints of the origins of Mrs Iron Mask being from Sussex. Sometimes she is referred to as Mrs Mason, therefore the wife of the alias that the 'Iron Mask' took at the trial in Bexleyheath.

At the end of September one local newspaper refers to a reward of a hundred pounds being offered to unmask the walker. Then by early October, mentions of his wife stop in the local newspaper reports. The caravan is nowhere to be seen and he is walking only with his assistant.

According to the McNaught family archive, Mable Reed goes back to her home town of Steyning in Sussex and in December 1908 she gives birth to a boy. He is christened 'Henry Claude Beasley' and she apparently names herself as Mrs Mabel Beasley on the birth certificate. It is possible that Harry is at his aliases again and it looks as though he had told his new 'wife' another lie. It is a small point but we can note that every alias he has made up uses the same initials HB, apart that is from the one used in Court in Bexleyheath, which was Henry Mason.

In a newspaper article in Northampton, the 'Iron Mask' names Lord Lonsdale in connection with the wager but does not say in what way he is connected.

In Wolverhampton, after nearly 2400 miles of walking the trail goes cold only for a remarkable article to appear in 'Answers' magazine in early December. In this article the writer describes how he was in prison when he read about the 'Man in the Iron Mask' and the idea for the whole enterprise came to him in a flash. It is a very detailed article and it may well be the most complete description of the entire hoax. It must have been written by the person who had inhabited the iron mask. Unfortunately, the article is anonymous and thus fails to prove that Harry Bensley was the Iron Mask.

Further doubt is cast on the possibility of Harry's involvement when the date of the Old Bailey trial is considered. It was November 16th, 1904 and Harry was sentenced to four years penal servitude. That would leave him languishing in gaol for the entire period that the Iron Mask was on the road.

It was time to don the coat and sift through the papers on Pentonville Prison at the National Archive in Kew, where I found that release dates are in fact not recorded, so it was impossible to confirm when Harry was freed. What the researchers were able to confirm is that prison overcrowding was a serious issue at this time and that typically prisoners would be released on license after three quarters of their sentence was complete (I am unable to find a reference for this and would instead have to refer you to the National Archive and the anecdotal experience of their researchers). If that had happened in Harry Bensley's case, then he would have been released on the 16th November 1907, perhaps just giving him enough time to put together the plan to start on the 1st January 1908. It would also mean that when he was arrested at Bexleyheath, he would have been in contravention of the terms of his license and would likely have been sent back to prison. On the other hand, if he was not released before the start of the walk then clearly, Harry Bensley was not the Iron Mask.

Is it possible that a third party could have been the Iron Mask? The answer has to be, yes. Indeed it is possible to plot any number of scenarios. For example, an anonymous walker was instructed by Harry Bensley in prison to begin the walk and his journey was overseen by his German benefactor. Later on, having been freed from prison, Harry Bensley meets the anonymous walker and because takings are falling he stops the walk and acquires the perambulator and other paraphernalia which much later he uses as a way of making money on the beaches of Essex. Here is another example, the anonymous walker changes his name either by accident or design to Harry Bensley to escape his past. Beyond the mere issue of how this might happen there are also the implications for Mabel Reed and Jim Beasley should the Iron Mask turn out to be a third party.

These would be amazing stories but before I get carried away I have to acknowledge that there is absolutely no evidence for any of them. However to muddy the waters even further here are two anecdotes from 'Wivenhoe – its attractions, Pleasures and Eccentric Natives' by Dick Barton, given by women who had met Harry Bensley. Mrs Hilda Abraham told the author, 'He was a bit of a mystery. He told us once that Harry Bensley was not his real name.' Meanwhile Mrs Alexandra Butt recalled, 'Bensley was an artful dodger. He said he had done everything under the sun except murder.'

I do believe in the context of this book that these two comments are more revealing than Harry Bensley intended. Harry has had many names and it is true that he got into more mischief than his claimed aristocratic past would have suggested. However we should not get carried away with this train of thought because this is how Harry creates the confusion so he can spin his tales.

So returning to the facts, I would suggest that the question is not whether Harry Bensley is the Iron Mask, it is which Harry Bensley, the aristocratic walker, the reckless gambler and womaniser or the fraudster and bigamist? Which one of these personas was actually inside the Mask?

Was he born to a large country house with a significant income? Did he go on to live in London and have a lavish lifestyle? I can find no facts to corroborate this story so the aristocratic Harry Bensley is unlikely to have been the man in the mask. This does rule out the reckless gambler narrative as well.

There is one clue to the identity of the person inside the mask. The opening words of the Answers magazine article are:

'Thank you my Lord, I deserve it.'

Four years earlier, journalists reported that Harry Bensley had used almost those exact words at the end of his Old Bailey trial:

'Thank you my Lord, I have deserved it'.

The words are not exactly the same but many a journalist would be happy with this evidence, there being two independent sources. I therefore put it to you that it is most likely that the writer of the anonymous article in Answers magazine and the prisoner found guilty of fraud and bigamy in the Old Bailey dock are one and the same.

It's not quite a proof, though.

News of the Iron Mask

THE BOGUS HEIR AND THE BARMAID

Wearing gold-rimmed eye-glasses, a weak faced young man without a collar stood in the dock before the Common Serjeant at the Old Bailey, yesterday. He was Harry Bensley, known as 'the bogus heir,' who was charged with obtaining large sums of money by fraud and also on two counts of bigamy. Whilst admitting the false pretences, Bensley denied the bigamy.

The evidence disclosed a remarkable story. Mr Bodkin told how the prisoner was married in Thetford, Norfolk and came to London to live, working as a labourer. In July 1902, he deserted his wife and children and married a Miss Lily Chapman (sic), a barmaid at a Norwood public-house. Bensley posed as the son and heir of "Sir Robert Burrell, Mayor of Thetford" – a person who did not exist. The prisoner said he would come into £12,000 and thousands of acres of land and persuaded a Mr Thomas Jordan and a Mr Sydney Bradley, both men in humble circumstances, to let him have £300 and £70 respectively – their life savings.

Miss Chapman (sic) – a sad faced lady in black, who is now a dressmaker, told how she met the prisoner. He was then a carman but he told her he expected to 'come into his estate in three years' time.'

Mr Matthews (who appeared with Mr Bodkin): Did he say where his estate was?

Witness: Yes, between Suffolk and Norfolk. (Laughter.)

In the statement he handed to the Judge, Bensley said he was not guilty of bigamy, for his wife had deserted him. He fell 'passionately in love with Miss Chapman (sic) at first sight' and thought he was doing no wrong in marrying her.

The jury, finding the prisoner guilty, he was sentenced to four years penal servitude on each of the three indictments, the sentences to run concurrently.

'Thank you, my lord, I have deserved it' – he remarked as he went out.
Yorkshire Telegraph, November 17, 1904

THE GREAT MASKED MAN HOAX

Our readers will doubtless remember that on Thursday, September 3 last, a man wearing an iron mask, and wheeling a perambulator, visited Ludlow on what was described as a walk round the world for a wager of £21,000 and his visit aroused much interest and curiosity.

In this week's "Answers" the individual in question relates the whole story of what was in fact an astounding fraud, and we reprint the article: –

Scene 1. – The Old Bailey.

Prisoner (sentenced to penal servitude): 'Thank you my Lord. I deserve it.'

(Interval of three years)

Scene 2. – The Mayor of R________'s house

The Mayor (to the Man in the Iron Mask): 'I am very glad to see you. You are the most illustrious person I have met this year. Please take a chair.'

WHAT GAVE ME THE IDEA

Incredible though it may sound the man in the felon's dock at the Central Criminal Court and the Mayor of R________'s guest were one and the same person – a brief extract from whose autobiography is now, for the first time, given to the public.

In the lonely hours of my prison life my thoughts often dwelt upon the future. I had been brought up to no trade and I had no business experience. While the unskilled labour market was glutted. And so I realised the fact that I must rely on my own efforts and this led to me to consider upon the best way by which I might get a living.

The time of my release from prison was drawing near when one day I found on returning to my cell that my library books had been changed.

I took up one of the volumes and glancing listlessly through its pages I saw that one of its articles was headed "The Mystery of the Iron Mask."

HOW I "FAKED" THE WAGER

That night my thoughts kept reverting to the "Man in the Iron Mask," till, in idle fancy I began to draw mental pictures of myself passing through life with an iron mask over my face. Gradually they took shape and substance and I began to evolve a scheme by means of which I could make a source of considerable profit. I thought of several plans till at last I hit upon the idea of walking round the world for a bogus wager. Needless to say, a mask was to be the chief feature of the scheme.

I spent the remaining weeks of my imprisonment perfecting my plans, writing each detail over and over again on my slate – the terms of the supposed wager and the conditions imposed. The walk was represented to be the outcome of a sporting wager of £21,000 between an English nobleman and an American millionaire, in which the former backed me to walk round the world wearing an iron mask and wheeling a child's ordinary perambulator. I was to support myself on the road only by what I could make from the sale of my pamphlets and picture post-cards of myself in the iron mask.

I was released from prison in November, 1907, with a gratuity of thirty shillings, which represented my sole worldly possession. I required at least £5 to open the campaign.

Immediately on my discharge from Pentonville I bought a large map of the British Isles, some foolscap and other trifling articles of stationery. I then proceeded to Clarkson's, the well-known theatrical costumers, where I inspected several masks, finally selecting one which was priced at twenty-five shillings. It was more than I could pay, and so I had to leave it for the time. I then took a train for the country town where my wife was living and I lost no time in making it known that a gentleman wished me to take up the job of walking round the world. Of course I enlarged upon the terms of the wager, and the conditions and restrictions imposed, mentioning incidentally that I had to provide the mask and perambulator myself, as the gentleman would not trust me with any money. Gossip soon bruited the matter amongst my neighbours, one of whom for a future consideration agreed to provide the perambulator.

I had occasion to come up to London one day and there I met with an old prison acquaintance. He was a German – a man of superior education and evidently of some social standing. In the course of conversation, the subject of the wager cropped up and, in a sudden burst of confidence, I told him the whole truth. To my surprise he offered to finance me, adding also he willingness to help me in any other way. And this I must say, he subsequently did by impersonating the English nobleman.

Of course the offer to help me was not a disinterested one on his part, and while I could not reasonably regret the money I had to give him from time to time, nevertheless, I found this gentleman a heavy tax on my takings.

SOME OF MY "DODGES"

I went home with the twenty-five shilling mask and at once ordered a moderate supply of pamphlets and postcards. It was necessary that the mask and the perambulator should be repainted and inscribed with advertisement slips and there were other expenses I had to incur. To meet these demands I fell back on an old dodge – it is as ancient as Adam – and got £5 by way of security from a young man I engaged to accompany me on my walk. In lieu of wages I proposed to give him £7,000 – a third of the £21,000 – on the successful completion of the walk but should he leave my service of his own will at any time before the expiration of six months from the date of his engagement, he was to forfeit the £5 security, except in the event of falling ill.

At length the day arrived – January 1st – which was to inaugurate the great wager. One of the conditions I forgot to mention was that I should find a "wife on the road." I already had a wife and intended getting her to join me as soon as I could provide suitable conveyance for her use.

On the morning of our "opening day", after an early breakfast, we chartered a four-wheeler and drove to the station. It was very foggy so that we attracted no attention on the way, although I was then masked. On our arrival at the station I stepped out of the cab and made at once

*for the London train, while my assistant ran the perambulator towards
the luggage van. But though the "Man in the Mask" – to his temporary
relief – had been allowed to pass unnoticed the perambulator was not
so fortunate. The stationmaster's eagle eye fell upon it and he asked me
if we had a ticket for it.*

*I was halfway across the platform when I turned around to see what
was the matter and in a second of time I found myself in the midst of
an excited crowd. For a minute I felt horribly nervous but the business
side of the arrangement helped me to pull myself together and I started
selling postcards for all I was worth. Passengers, porters, the guard,
even the stationmaster were among my eager customers. Perhaps it
would be safe to say that, in this station at least, articles were for the
first time allowed to be peddled on the platform.*

*We reached Charing Cross about ten o'clock. Just before 10.30 which
had been announced for the commencement of the walk, a
representative of the "Daily Mirror" photographed us, and immediately
we started our walk "through the world," proceeding by way of the
Strand to Cheapside, and then over London Bridge to Woolwich, selling
the cards and pamphlets as fast as we could take the money.*

MY LITTLE WALKING TRIP

*The fog by this time had cleared and every street on our route was
thronged with excited crowds of people. The novelty of my position,
the press of customers for cards, the noise of the traffic, completely
bewildered me, for I was unable at the close of the day to recall any
particular incident that had occurred. It was all a blur of faces, a
monotone of meaningless sound. We did not taste a mouthful of food, or
even a drop of water from the time we had our breakfast, 7.30 'till 9.30
in the evening.*

*Since then our itinerary has been chronicled daily in the provincial
press. During the last ten months I have walked over 2,400 miles,
visited the principal cities and towns in England and South Wales.
From Penzance to Wolverhampton and even from Swansea to
Lowestoft, meeting everywhere with enthusiastic receptions. But*

before I close my narrative I may be allowed to refer incidentally to the hoax I was forced to play on the majesty of the law.

It was arranged that my assistant should sell the cards and pamphlets, for which he had been provided with the requisite license while I was merely to exhibit myself masked and wheel the perambulator. I was standing in Bexley Heath when a small boy came up and holding a coin in his hand, asked me for a card. Without giving him a thought I handed him the card and took the money. I was at once arrested for peddling without a licence, and brought before the local magistrate.

In view of the terms of my supposed wager, these gentlemen, with great consideration, allowed me to appear in court without uncovering. I suppose it is the only incidence where a prisoner has been tried and sentenced with his headgear un-doffed. I regretted the necessity which forced me to take such a step but if I had removed the mask, the "wager" would have collapsed.

WHY I THREW UP THE SPONGE

Since then I have been wearing this helmet daily for ten months – a weight of 4lbs. 5oz. I have wheeled the perambulator – which weighted 1cwt. 1lb. – a distance of 2,400 miles. The strain began to tell upon me. My eyes ached and I suffered with racking pains in my head. On several occasions I fainted by the roadside and sometimes I was even confined to bed for two or three days at a stretch. And then my wife insisted that I should give up the walk. I should like to have continued with it but circumstances were too strong for me. I had to cancel arrangements I had made to appear at several music halls when I left Wolverhampton a few weeks ago.

In conclusion, I can assert, without fear of contradiction, that I have paid my way and supported myself, my wife and my assistant, the horses and attendants, I employed entirely from the sale of my cards and pamphlets and that I have received nothing in the shape of charity from the first day of my itinerary.

The Ludlow Advertiser, December 19, 1908

Some assumptions

This is a fictionalised account and I have taken some liberties where there were no facts to be followed. Also in order to motivate certain storylines I have made some assumptions based upon the actions of Harry and Kate.

I don't know when they met or how they met or why they split up. I do know they got back together again and I *wanted to believe* that Kate was his firm companion until his death. So my first assumption is, that despite everything that happened between them at the beginning of the twentieth century, they loved each other very much.

When Harry split up with Kate in 1901 his movements are thoroughly reported by both the press and the transcript of the court case in the Old Bailey. Frankly, there is a massive dichotomy between the depiction of Harry Bensley in the newspapers as a criminal mastermind and the reality of the doubt-ridden defendant in the box at the Old Bailey. For example, his threats to his second wife to commit suicide and indeed his alleged attempt are very much at odds with the personality of the smooth talking confidence trickster popularised by the press. In fleeing the country, what was he running from? From justice? From his previous life? From the mess he had made? Again there are no answers on the record so it is difficult to tell exactly why he did these things but I have made one assumption based upon his actions. That assumption is that he suffered from mild bipolar disease and when he was with Kate somehow he kept the disease at bay but once he was on his own, he lost control completely. While he was in a manic phase, he could be irrepressibly charming to men and women alike. When he was in a depressive phase he could want to run and hide away, have severe panic attacks or even contemplate suicide. It could well be that the epileptic fit that took him to Stepney Infirmary in 1901 was in fact a panic attack. I will say that this is my speculation and I used it purely to motivate the narrative and did not put it into the story. The closest anyone gets to this diagnosis is the German prisoner who I have called Torben Maier who considers it a mania. This is new-fangled thinking as Jung had only just described this diagnosis a year earlier. To be fair, it would be an unusual presentation of bipolar disease, one that was calmed by proximity to his wife, which is why I make no mention of it in the text.

From the Answers magazine article we find the only mention of the German prisoner who was to fund his enterprise. There is not enough information to track this man down (I have tried with no success) but without doubt he is very important to the story and I have therefore greatly enlarged his role in this narrative.

In Answers magazine, the anonymous writer describes reading an article about 'The Man in the Iron Mask'. I take this further by suggesting that he read the book. This is the last in the Musketeers series by Dumas and a dark end for D'Artagnan, Porthos and Athos with only the wily Aramis surviving by the last chapter. I fancy that Harry sees himself as D'Artagnan, favourite of the King, riding out to public acclaim behind the mask. I also fancy that Harry thinks of the German fellow ('Torben' in the book) as Porthos his loyal companion but as Harry continues the challenge he revises his opinion and starts to believe that Torben is much more in the mould of the dangerous and scheming Aramis, seizing the opportunity for personal enrichment before friendship. He is mistaken though.

My final assumption was that Harry and Kate was a love story which begins at the beginning and ends at the end. It is how I first envisaged the story, the love of a good, true and honest woman saves him. So it is with much sadness that I have to write the next few paragraphs.

The first chink in the story was on the McNaught website. They claimed that their investigations had uncovered Kate as being a piano teacher from Manchester. I was ready to ignore this observation and class it as an outlier as it did not match up with the record of births, marriages and deaths. However much later I was checking the references for this book and I found a passage in 'Wivenhoe –

its attractions, pleasures and eccentric natives' by Dick Barton, that described his wife Kate as a 'north country woman'. Whatever people in Wivenhoe may say about Suffolk folk, it would be an extraordinary act of geographic pedantry to describe them as northerners and the fact that Harry and Kate lived prominently in the town for nearly eighteen years strongly suggests that this Kate was not his first wife.

The inevitable conclusion is that the Kate at his side when Harry died in Brighton in 1956 was probably not the same Kate who married him in 1898.

Which would make a lot of sense because the anonymous writer in the Answer's magazine article states that he returned to his wife at the end of the walk, after 'throwing up the towel' as he called it in Wolverhampton. Within weeks, the warts and all admission of his great hoax, as it was titled was in print. My personal belief is that the article appeared because Kate, his first wife, required him to write it as part of the price for his return to the family home. Admittedly this is my speculation but the form is that Harry Bensley, when cornered, is a man who admits his guilt.

Taking this into account the idea that after the war his first wife Kate would be untroubled by Harry telling all and sundry his remarkable tall tale does not really make any sense. I find it very unlikely that he would have kept all of his paraphernalia, the perambulator, helmet and even some negatives of the postcards sold along the route. That being said, I was ready to believe that he might have won Kate round to the idea when finances became tight, especially during the great depression.

However Dick Barton's book tells us that he arrived and departed as the Man who walked round the world but for the intervention of the Great War and I find it difficult to believe that Kate, his first wife, would have allowed it.

The documentation shows that Harry, after being released from the army did not go back to his previous home but took up residence in Catford. Dick Barton's book says that Harry told people that after leaving the army, he then worked at Woolwich Arsenal. Harry is a terrible source to take at face value (see the rest of this book for details) but I personally believe that he did not go back to his family and probably he met his new Kate, if that was her real name, during this time.

As to the final fate of his first wife, I can offer no details. There is no death certificate in her name and no record of a divorce or subsequent marriage. I only hope that when the next census records are available it will be possible to find some trace of her. I will certainly continue with my investigations in case this story needs a further chapter.

I will admit that I came to this conclusion very late, after I was rechecking information for the references and I spotted the 'north country woman' quote.

Acknowledgments

I first met Harry Bensley in an article in my local paper, the Essex County Standard on December 4, 2015 titled 'Mystery man walked round the world and ended up in Essex'. I read it and then put it to one side thinking I would be interested to know more about this incredible feat and when I had some spare time I would look into it. Harry had piqued my interest and as a keen walker I was very impressed by the idea of someone walking around the world and amazed that I had never heard of Harry Bensley's adventure before.

There are two websites on the internet where I began my investigations. The first is the official Harry Bensley website which is maintained by the descendants of Harry Bensley's road wife Mabel Reed. Known as the McNaught family website, they tell the main story and the secret regarding the gambling debt. They have amassed a large archive of original material, including photographs, postcards and transcripts of items such as the pamphlet that was sold along the way. I am deeply indebted to them.

A couple of notes of caution though. Firstly there is no actual proof that Mabel Reed and Harry Bensley were ever together. The best that can be said is that the Iron Mask's companion is reported in some newspaper articles to be a lady from Steyning in Sussex. There are also photographs that do show a lady with the group that the family say is Mabel Reed. As I have already mentioned the records also show that her death was recorded in her married name of Mabel Lillian Kemp in 1926.

Secondly there is the son, Jim, who is supposed to have visited Harry in the Brighton hospital. He was, according to the family, christened Henry Claude Beasley and was the son of a Mabel Beasley. But where the name Jim came from, where the name Beasley came from and whether he was the son of Harry Bensley and indeed (dare

I say it) whether he actually met Harry Bensley in Brighton, is unfortunately a matter for speculation.

This does make me sound as though I doubt every word of it which is far from my design, rather I want to show just how many holes there are in all the strands of this particular story.

A second website known as the Big Retort is run by a freelance investigative reporter JP Brodie. His motto seems to be 'trust nobody' and he has a lot of fun trashing the original story. He uncovered much of the felonious past of Harry Bensley and I am greatly in debt for his research on the Old Bailey Trial. I must note that he was the first to unearth the Answers magazine article. His scepticism about Harry Bensley and indeed any and every aspect of his story was a massive driving force for this book.

After reading these desperately contradictory sources I began my own investigation into the facts. The rest of the research was undertaken using the websites of Ancestry, Find My Past and Genes Reunited. I viewed documents at the offices of the National Archives at Kew and the London Metropolitan Archives in Clerkenwell. I was checking dates of birth, marriage, death and census records constantly. While also sifting through court, army, prison and workhouse records.

I very quickly learnt that just because a document can be viewed or held, this is not proof of its veracity.

The newspaper archives were very problematic from this point of view. The news reports had to be read with a significant amount of caution, especially as the Iron Mask generated thousands of articles. However I am indebted to the various newspaper archives run by Genes Reunited in particular.

I must thank the Old Bailey website for the précis of the 1904 trial of Harry Bensley for fraud and bigamy.

I tried to ensure that any weather events were actual and extend my grateful thanks for the monthly weather summaries on the Met Office website. The snow storm on the South coast was a real event and must have caused Harry much misery as he covered the section from Portsmouth to Weymouth. I also wanted to be sure that the August Bank Holiday weekend on Clacton-on-Sea beach was on record as a scorcher.

I must mention one man who must have a lot of spare time on his hands and that is Tim Kirby. He has painstakingly found news articles and other items and placed them on a dynamic map that covers the whole known route which can be seen on the McNaught family website. It might not look much but I know having vainly tried to search these archives that there are literally thousands of articles, the majority of which are merely syndicated copies and very rarely did I find an original source. When I did it was as if I had found gold dust, especially when there was an interview with Mr Iron Mask. Tim Kirby's research effectively doubled the number of articles that I had access to in which the Iron Mask is interviewed and these interviews were instrumental in forming much of the character of the man in the mask.

Prior to the actual event according to the Answers Magazine article, the Iron Mask bought the knight's helmet from Clarkson's theatrical costumiers. The proprietor was Willie Clarkson, an extraordinary man, whose real life crossed both the theatrical and criminal worlds. I based Willie Clarkson's character upon an article entitled 'London's Perruquiers' which was mainly an interview with the owner printed in the weekly theatrical newspaper 'The Era' in November 1900. I am grateful to Arthur Lloyd's music hall and theatre history website for bringing this to my attention. The site of Clarkson's shop, the clock and plaques for the coping stones laid by Sarah Bernhardt and Sir Henry Irving can still be seen at 41-43 Wardour Street.

'The Norfolk turnippe' and 'To be a farmer's boy' are traditional Norfolk folk songs.

'The Galloping Major' was a famous music hall standard of 1906 written and composed by Fred W. Leigh & George Bastow.

In my other life as a film maker I am always aware that a programme can be improved and listen closely, without ego, to any criticism. It has been harder to take criticism as an author. Without a team of fellow collaborators I feel much more protective of my project but I have tried to stay open to the opinions of others.

There are many things I would like to believe that I know are not true. For example, I would like to believe that I am a natural writer, but my writing in its rawest form is filled with mixing-my-tenses and other fatal grammatical errors. Irritants that can be toxic to the more sensitive reader. Therefore the painstaking work of the editor was crucial to finesse the final product. In this I was doubly blessed as my lifelong friend Chris Priest took on the task and his hard work and honest appraisal has made this book what it is today.

I would also like to thank Harriet Paige, author of 'Man with a Seagull on His Head.' Listening to her experiences on the long road to becoming a published author the one message Harriet was keen to impart was 'write the best book you can'. It is a simple and inspiring thought for any author.

One of my most helpful and evocative objects was a postcard that I bought on eBay. It is one of the very first souvenirs of the Iron Mask and his assistant, which was taken at Lepard Studios in Croydon, most probably prior to the start on New Year's day. Sadly it was never posted, so there is no record of where the purchaser met the Iron Mask. It does not matter. I hold it when I have lost my thread and the knowledge that at some time in the past it must have been in the perambulator and handled by either the Iron Mask or his assistant has spurred me on to complete this book.

Or maybe this book is not complete because there are many other postcards hidden in antique shops, boot sales and attics just waiting to be discovered. Perhaps you will find the one that suggests he did walk further?

Finally, this is a fictionalised account and if I have made any errors or omissions then I respectfully ask for your forgiveness. However, with a subject such as Harry Bensley, how can you be sure of anything?